D1232356

Confidence Unlocked

By Kiawana Leaf

© 2019

ALL RIGHTS RESERVED. No part of this book may be reproduced in any written, electronic, recording, or photocopying without written permission of the publisher or author. The exception would be in the case of brief quotations embodied in the critical articles or reviews and pages where permission is specifically granted by the publisher or author.

PUBLISHED BY: Pen Legacy® (penlegacy.com)
TYPESETTING & LAYOUT BY: Junnita Jackson
(www.theliarscraft.com)
STORY EDITING BY: U Can Mark My Word Editorial Services

DISCLAIMER

Although you may find the teachings, life lessons and examples in this book to be useful, the book is sold with the understanding that neither the co-authors nor Pen Legacy, LLC. are engaged in presenting any legal, relationship, financial, emotional, or health advice.

Any person who's experiencing financial, anxiety, depression, health, or relationship issues should consult with a licensed therapist, advisor, licensed psychologist, or any qualified professional before commencing into anything described in this book. This book's intent is to provide you with the writer's account and experience with overcoming life matters. All results will differ; however, our goal is to provide you with our "take" on how to overcome and be resilient when faced with circumstances. There are lessons in every blessing.

Library of Congress Cataloging – in- Publication Data has been applied for.

ISBN: 978-0-9961880-1-1
PRINTED IN THE UNITED STATES OF AMERICA

Introduction

She was a good girl, but too many undermining scenarios had turned her life upside down. My biggest flaw seemed to be having a big heart! Have you ever been in a situation that awakens your soul, directing you to pay attention and self-evaluate yourself? Ever felt utterly empty, numb, and didn't know what to do, where to turn, or possibly even who to turn to? Do you find yourself perpetuating after having experienced many storms? Remaining independent, strong, and always wearing a smile, but deep inside, you want to break down? Fully understanding having to laugh to keep from crying? Have endured mental, physical, and emotional abuse? Feel like the world is against you rather than with you? Fear judgment from church, so instead, you don't go? Wonder why he or she does certain things to you? Wonder what love is exactly? Has the church hurt you? Do you find yourself asking God why or questioning your purpose? Feel like no one understands you but are quick to judge you? Have questions formed from pain and wondering how to sustain?

Confidence Unlocked gets raw and authentic, sharing my discoveries during my life's journey, and is broken into three parts: *my TESTimony, Healing, and Process*. I hope and pray that you will be blessed, inspired, and encouraged after reading my story!

Inspiration

I just want to Inspire
The ones that are fed up and tired
Hold your head high
The sky is the limit
No reason to walk around timid
Know your worth or no one else will
They'll do anything in their power to keep you still
Shine bright, don't ever let them dim you
You are who God calls you
And no one can steal this

I'm trying to smile through my pain
You left my heart with a stain
Can you really be the one to blame?
I gave all the signs it was a game
It was okay to raise your hand
I'm no longer taking a stand
But you're supposed to be my man
I'd do anything that I can
No longer was it a game
You're constantly doing the same
My life is precious
I'm generous
Sacrifice my last to make you smile
It seems like a test
That I'm barely able to pass
Now here I am drowning in my sorrows
Putting on a front, looking forward to tomorrow

You are a Queen
Don't ever settle for anything less
I made a mistake and failed the test
I am a Queen
I will never settle for anything less
I just want to Inspire!
Girl, you're worth an empire
It's time to heal and share my story

I

She's one trying to find herself. A 26-year-old woman born in Silver Spring, Maryland, and raised in Uptown DC, she has experienced a tragic situation. She is now wondering what's her purpose and looking for healing from God. In addition to being a mother of one, she's a daughter, a sister, a friend, and a survivor! Most importantly, she's a child of God!

I guess you're wondering who is *she*. She is me – Kiawana, or Key as I'm called by those who are closest to me, a beautiful woman that the world sees. When I looked in the mirror, I saw insecurities, fear, doubt, brokenness, hatred, toxicity, questions, confusion, and chaos. Can you relate to me?

Born June 15, 1991, and the prettiest Gemini baby, I am my parents' joy. The gift of life alone is a blessing. I am a miracle, and yes, so are you!

After graduating from high school, I went on to complete cosmetology school and enrolled in college but didn't finish my first year. I was in private schools during my younger years and even attended church school where I met some phenomenal people, created indescribable bonds, and most importantly, was introduced to Christ. I've been attending church since in mother's womb. I became accustomed to it, and it became part of my weekly schedule. However, I grew apart from the church as I grew older.

You see, I have been in the most damaging, abusive relationships that you could think of: mentally, physically, verbally, and emotionally. All the pain I endured became part of my healing. My life started to change, and as it changed, I began to feel judgment from the church. It seemed that to be a Christian, you had to portray a certain image or be part of a clique just to fit in. I feared being judged by the church members or should I say by the leadership. I didn't want my life to become their next topic of gossip. This is *my* journey -- *my* confidence unlocked!

I thank God for my life, health, and strength. If you know all that I've been through, you would think He should've taken life from me a long time ago, but if He had, how would I be able to tell my story? He saw fit to call me to be a vessel to share my purpose, just as He is strengthening you to fulfill yours! I always wondered, *Why am I still here?* *Why am I going through hell and back? God, what is my purpose? Why me?* Have you ever felt this way or had those questions? If so, you are not alone. If not, don't judge me. I'm just being me!

II

At two years old, what does a child really know about friendship? Yet, the two of us instantly clicked. By four years old, we gained another good girlfriend. Then, I developed an incredible relationship with my third best friend in kindergarten. I don't remember much about this age, but indeed, I had three best friends. We all went to the same school, and my mother along with the parents of two of my friends worked at our school as a registrar, principal, and teacher! However, one of my friends left shortly after preschool and another after completing kindergarten. Still, we all remained connected since our families attended the same church.

One of the best times of my life was while in elementary school. As children, we had no worries. We were so pretty in our beautiful dresses and ruffled socks, with bows and ribbons adorning our long ponytails. Carefree spirits, we were silly, anointed, and unaware of our callings. During chapel day service, we'd get drenched in anointing oil, have hands laid on us, and prayers spoken over us! Because we were young, we didn't fully grasp what was going on and didn't fully understand a covering. Still, back then, it was the time of my life. I had no worries about being under attack, fighting off demons and evil spirits, or winning battles. I was simply living.

My childhood was really amazing; I can say I've truly been blessed. My mother didn't have a lot, but she made it the best for me. As a child, you don't really pay attention to how blessed you really are, but as the years pass, you start to realize it more.

As I got older, my friendship circle grew. I created a sisterhood, a deep bond with my girls. I also would like to mention that no one had better sleepovers than us! (smile) Aside from my childhood being fun, it was also when I first started experiencing minor insecurity issues. Of course, kids being kids, the bullying began. A short, stubby, round little girl, I remember being teased because of my weight, but rather than crumbling while being ridiculed, I began building my inner strength. Sure, there were many times when I wanted to break down and cry, but instead, I'd give the sassiest attitude any little girl could ever give in return. Let us tell it, we were the cool kids. (chuckle)

We created some unforgettable memories! My friends and I did what most kids our age liked to do back then — had sleepover, played on the chat line, made prank calls, and talked about boys. Some of the school activities and groups that we participated in were the cheerleading team, step team, "Daughters of Destiny", spirit week, twin day, field trips, and yes, even visits to the principal's office, which was not a good thing, especially since the principal was the dad one of my friends. I can even recall the time we repainted my friend's basement. Just laughter, tears, and conversation shared amongst close friends!

#STRONGFORKAYLA

It was 1994 when we first met
Everything was literally the best
From church to school
Barely able to tie our own shoes
Sleepovers to clubs
Before we knew it, we were a dub
My girl, my sister, nothing will ever differ
Talks about toys to boys
Our bond was something hard to destroy
Up all night on the phone
Talking about God knows what
We were tight
No matter what, the heart was right
Why, God? Why my sister?
Are you there? Are you even listening?
This pain here is something different
I'm yelling and screaming
I'm letting the phone keep ringing
Arguing and fighting
Seems our relationship is really ending
What? No never!
That's not clever
We are better than that
Argue to fight? Girl, we're better than that
No more fuss and fights

I love you and that's my life
Patched up the fixings
Our relationship is different
In the middle of the night, I'll never forget
It's a few calls that I missed
2017, they told me God called you home
I just can't believe it
How could He do this to me
I can't stop these tears from flowing
This news here is torment
My heart skips a few beats while I try to breathe
I'm crying, screaming, and can't fall back to sleep
Man, this here is deep
They say God doesn't make mistakes
But this right here, I really can't take
Laying my childhood to rest
God, is this some kind of test
We only want for the best
But this here went left
I hear the waves flowing
Our mermaid is finally soaring
I feel you with me; I know your presence is there
You're living with us; you'll always be there
Kay, you are finally healed
I just wasn't prepared
We've repaired but weren't able to rebuild
One of the hardest and still try to live
One sweet day we'll reunite again
Until that day, I promise to walk my purpose
So, when that day comes, God will tell me
You've completed your test; you finally can rest

And I will completely be healed so we can meet again
I miss and love you forever, my sister!

III

I've always longed for the love of my father. I wanted to be a daddy's girl, for him to be my best friend and someone who I idolized. I wanted my father to be an example of the type of men I should date. I wanted my husband–and even my unborn son–to be like my daddy. I wanted to hold my father's hand. I imagined him always being there for every step I took, kissing away the pain of every bruise and heartbreak, supporting and celebrating my every accomplishment. I wanted to be daddy's baby girl. My best friends had their fathers present in their lives, and I envied their beautiful bond because it's the type of relationship I dreamed of having with my father. Not having it took a toll on me.

There's always two sides to a story, but do either really matter when the child should be the priority? Despite wanting to have a bond with my father, I had to accept that it would more than likely never happen. Seeing him every other weekend—or whenever he felt like he wanted to be bothered––wasn't good enough for me. As I grew older, I became accustomed to not having a close relationship with my dad.

When it came to him, my attitude was *it is what it is*.

My stepfather became my father figure, and in my eyes, he was the best. Still, he wasn't my dad. Isn't it every girl's dream to be spoiled and loved by their father. Instead, it seemed mine was stingy and only concerned about himself, which is the opposite of what I wished he would be.

Now, as an adult, I'm looking for my father's love in all the wrong places. I'm gullible; I mistake lust for love. But, how can I know what's the proper way for a man to love me when I never had the example of love from my father. Would things have been different if I had such an example? For those fathers who are not in their child's life, do they understand the significance of their presence in the child's life and the harm it does to the child when they are not?

In my case, I yearned for a father's love but failed to search for love from my Father above. Instead, I grew bitter. I wasn't desperate to seek love from my Father above but rather from my father here on earth, and it left my heart scorned.

Through the years, things have been distant between my father and me. Even now, things aren't that very different. I wanted nothing more than to let go of the past and start things anew. I sought his opinion and wanted to share with him about whoever I was dating. These things should have been easy, but with him, it seemed like the most difficult thing to do. Then whenever I expressed myself to my father, he would say I was being too grown and disrespectful, not seeing how my heart was torn. Whether your child is a boy or a girl, a father's presence is needed in both genders' lives! There is only so much a mother can provide emotionally for her children, and a father's role in the child's life is just as imperative. Still, it seems they don't understand or maybe they just choose not to want to understand.

And for those mothers who use their children as pawns when it comes to their relationship with their child's father, stop it. If the father wants to be a part of their child's life, allow them in. The reason for the breakup between the two of you doesn't matter. It's no longer about you! It's about the well-being and happiness of the child that the two of you share together. We have to play our part and make the attempt to help build a bond between the father and child. If all else fails, leave it completely in the Lord's hands.

Daddy, the beginning was a mystery
It seemed there was no chemistry
So distant, yet so close to me
I wondered does Daddy have time for Key
They say things get worse before they get better
But, at this point, I'm really feeling fed up
Is there one to blame?
Things are really lame
But I continue to stay in my own lane
Fighting demons, enduring the pain
Is this forever or just a temporary stain?
Daddy, you are a great gift to me
I'm not the son you wished in me
But, Dad, some conversations are history
I build a bond off pain, you see
And, Dad, that's why you're a great gift to me
This bond wasn't just handed to me
I wish then things were different, but I just let it be
But, you're still here, and that's a gift to me

Part I
"TESTimony"
IV

As my father and I worked on building a better bond, my mom and I began to clash. Needing an escape, I would go to my dad's house, which he shared with his girlfriend. She could relate to me and ended up being a better person to talk to than my dad. She never judged me or denied me, but rather accepted me for me. She would let me express myself freely and tell me when I was wrong.

You see, I was at the age where I wanted do what I wanted. I started making bad choices when it came to friends, doing things I had no business doing, and running with the wrong crowd. Every parent's favorite line is, "You're smelling yourself." And, oh boy, was I! What I took as nagging was actually them showing love and concern for me. My mother's nagging is what caused us to start clashing. I thought she was being too hard on me and not giving me any room to grow into myself. I only wish I had listened before it was too late.

17

By my sophomore year, I was skipping classes and barely passing. Some girls in high school chose not to associate with me because of the company I kept, and as a result, I started to make more enemies while feeling like I had to defend myself. Eventually, my poor decisions led to me getting in a less than desirable situation with people who I "thought" were my friends, and I found myself sitting handcuffed in the back of the police car.

During the ride to the precinct, I started thinking to myself, *What's a friend to me?* Furthermore, I wondered, *How am I going to tell my parents? How am I going to get out of this? Am I really going to jail for this? Will I have to stay or will they let me go? This is really happening. What am I going to do?*

When one of the officers told me that the only way they would be able to release me is to contact my parents, I began to panic inside. *Contact my parents! That can't happen!* My mother was very stern and a strict disciplinarian; she didn't tolerate any mess. She would backhand me in the mouth for talking back and make me go get a belt from her room for my own whippings. And although I didn't have a tight connection with my father, I knew he was mean. So, there wasn't any doubt in my mind that I would get a good cursing out from him and probably a beating, too. My whole life, my dad had only beaten me once, and that was because I lied to him. Still, I didn't want to risk having to experience that wrath again. Therefore, I decided I would do whatever I had to do to keep them from finding out about the trouble that I was in.

Instead of having the authorities contact my parents, I gave them the phone number of one of my friends who I knew would pretend to be my mother. It worked! I was finally released. However, while on the train heading home, I started expcriencing butterflies in my stomach. I knew what I had done wasn't a clever idea, and I had a feeling it wasn't over.

When I got to school the following day, I got called to the principal's office. My feelings were right; it wasn't over. The police department informed my school of what I had done. Now, because I had the police call my friend instead of my mother, I was in more trouble than I would have been had I just been honest in the beginning.

Because of my violation, I was on the verge of getting expelled. I went back and forth, in and out of courts. Not just any courts, though. Virginia courts. Fighting for my freedom and to be able to stay in school sent my life for a twirl. "KIAWANA, THOSE ARE NOT YOUR FRIENDS!" was what my mother often told me. If only I would've listened when she first told me, but no, I wanted to do me. I wanted to fit in. I would have rather been accepted by my peers than listen to what was instilled in me.

Because of my disobedience, at the age of sixteen, I found myself facing my first offense and a criminal record that my mother and lawyers were fighting to get expunged. My mother, who was paying tuition for my high school education, fought so that the archdiocese didn't completely dismiss me. It was a battle the judge didn't see fit nor did my principal. What kind of example would I be setting? What type of image would they be displaying if they continued to let me attend the school? They were stern about making sure students learned their lesson, and they were determined to make me an example. What seemed so petty to me was beyond real to them! If convicted, I would be labeled a felon, and my mother would have to pay a substantial amount of money for legal fees. If I were to end up getting expelled from school, it would've been a waste of all that my mother sacrificed to keep me in private schools. Luckily, for me, I was only charged with a misdemeanor. I had to pay a minimum fine and perform several hours of community service. In exchange, my record was expunged. After being given another chance to stay enrolled at my school, I'm glad to be able to say I'm an alumna graduate of the Class of 2009.

I thought by "doing me" it made me grown, even though I knew that everything I was doing was wrong. My mother's "nagging" and the warning words that they were not my friends continued to reverberate in my mind. As I recall the feeling of the handcuffs tightly around my wrists, I finally get what she was saying. The law officials could look at me and tell I didn't belong, but they were adamant I learn that what I did was wrong and should never be done again. Skipping class to skipping school to truancy, to meetings with the principal and facing a judge to await his decision; all these things came about because of the so-called "friends" I had chosen.

I'm not fearful of my mess
I constantly celebrate the test
This molded me; it transformed me
A girl to a woman is my best story
Because God gets all my glory
Without this pain, would I still ask for You to restore me?

There's purpose in your pain
I finally get that saying
I don't feel no shame

But this isn't a story to frame
No fingers, no one to blame
Just watch how God restored me
To be able to tell my story
My story that's my testimony
So, excuse me while I storm please
This here is a new glow for me
I've gained my identity
I love the real Key

V

Do you remember back when BlackPlanet was poppin'? It was the best online site to meet people. One day, my friend showed me the profile of his cousin, some caramel-complexion boy who had big lips and dreads. Dreadheads were my type; they would get me every time!

The dreadhead and I exchanged phone numbers through my friend, who was our mutual connection. After some time of exchanging text messages back and forth, the two of us finally met in person, and he looked exactly like his pictures. Whenever I was with him, I would experience a feeling I had never felt before, and it didn't take long for us to become the best of friends. He gave me a shoulder to lean on whenever I needed one and showed me support. I had found a friend indeed. The first few months everything was going good, and that's to be expected when things are so new. After all, both parties have to make a good first impression, right? We became best friends and lovers. You wouldn't see one without the other. Even though we were both young, I thought he was it. I just knew he was going to be my husband, and we would have a family together. We both had been through so much and overcame most. Nothing could tear us apart…or so I thought. Boy, was I in for a rude awakening!

In 2008, during my junior year in high school, he and I would meet up at Brookland Station after school. We would go shopping, to dinner, the movies, Gallery Place, Union Station, Georgetown, or just spend time chilling. We had the perfect teenage love affair, but just like any other relationship, we had our basic problems. We would agree to disagree and break up to make up. Honestly, we were still kids trying to figure ourselves out.

By my senior year, we were still hanging on. However, I started evaluating our relations and asking myself some questions. Is this what we really want, or do we just like the idea of being together? Have we just gotten used to the date nights, late-night phone calls, texting throughout the day, and enjoying each other's company overall? Is it the benefits I like, or am I genuinely falling in love with this boy? Anytime something feels too good to be true you'll find yourself questioning the "realness" of it.

I felt complete; I felt loved. I received the time, attention, and nearly anything else I really wanted from him, and it made me feel good. I was being spoiled just like the daddy's little girl that I always wanted to be!

After graduating from high school, I decided not to go straight to college. Instead, I wanted to chase my dream and passion – cosmetology. I was accepted into Aveda Institute in DC. While I was attending school, he and I continued to spend time together. I was happy; I was content. We would go on lunch dates, wake up and go to sleep next to each other, and take trips together. He would shower me with Louis Vuitton bags and other materialistic things I wanted. I was living the life! Never did I question where he got all those finer things or how he was able to afford them. Nope! The only things I cared about was that I was in love, happy, and enjoying the time, attention, and support I was receiving from him. That's all I needed. The money and gifts were a bonus.

A lot of things started to change, though. I recognized the signs but ignored the flags. Random girls were calling and texting his phone late at night. Some were even so bold to send him naked pictures. He became more active on Myspace, getting caught up in the model girl scene. Clearly, I had some competition, but, he would brush off my concern by saying, "Them girls don't mean nothing to me. I'm always with you." His words started to sound like the lyrics of a broken record as I continued to receive more gifts and money.

However, the song became something I began to sing, too, as I made excuses for him. *I'm tripping. I get everything I want, so why should I be worried?* Those were the thoughts that crossed my mind. Yet, I started looking at myself differently in the mirror, and my feeling of insecurities resurfaced. I viewed myself as not being good enough or pretty enough. I wasn't the video vixen type that seemed to catch his eye. Like most other women, I would compare myself to the women who are seen on TV and who are most appealing to society today. My breasts aren't a picture-perfect portrait of perkiness, and I haven't spent thousands of dollars for cosmetic surgery to achieve a perfect body or flaunt a big butt, or phat ass as they like to refer to them nowadays. I don't smother my face with make-up daily to look a certain way. I tried to understand why there was such a sudden change in him, but after taking a closer look at myself, I could see that I wasn't part of the "society" that he was caught up in.

At this point, we had been together for almost three years. It's true that no relationship is perfect, but I was having a problem trying to figure out what were the imperfections of ours. *What is it? Is it someone else? What can I do to fix this?* I asked him so many questions, willing to change myself to fix him.

But then, I had to ask myself did our relationship really mean that much to me that I would be willing to drown just so he could swim. I started to realize that by being with him, I was turning myself into something I am not.

I can remember the time when we were in his mother's living room. That day, I saw a side of him that I had never seen before.

"Bitch, I'm not doing shit!" he had screamed and then forced me against the wall, his hands wrapped so tightly around my throat that I could hardly breathe. The red in his enraged eyes caused me to become very afraid.

Tears persistently flowed down my face as I experienced a rush of many emotions. I was hurt, angry, embarrassed, and felt betrayed. I didn't know how to react. Overall, my body was in shock! After he stormed out the door, his mother tried to console me, apologizing for her son's actions.

How would I tell my mother that he put his hands on me? What would people say about me? Even though I didn't have a close relationship with my father, I didn't want to chance telling him and have him respond in an act of violence towards my boyfriend. Telling my family wouldn't have been pretty. They are all crazy. Well, maybe I shouldn't use the word crazy. They are very protective of me. Not only my family but my elder male friends who consider me to be their little sister. This type of behavior they just wouldn't accept. Knowing this, I had to protect him, and I would do that by not letting them find out what had happened.

I started thinking I had overreacted and should've never questioned him. Yes, I became one of those women who make excuses for the man, faulting myself for his actions. Really, I did it in the mix of protecting him! That day, I didn't leave him. I made the decision to stay and sweep everything under the rug. After all, I loved him, but did I really know what love is?

In addition to his street dealings, my boyfriend was in the music industry. He would often leave, telling me that he had to go put in time at the studio or was going on tour. Sometimes he would stay gone for as long as two or three months, saying he was "handling business." Of course, he fed me those pacifying lines of "I love you," and "I miss you," while he kept the money coming in.

He told me that he got signed under the label Studio 43 and was working closely with Kenny Burns, who soon became my crush. However, whenever I asked him to tell me about the shows or to share the details of the music industry with me, he wouldn't respond. Glad to have my baby home with me, I wouldn't press him about it.

Although I appeared to be happy on the outside, I continued to experience flashbacks of what happened that day at his mother's house, constant reminders of his physical, emotional, and mental abuse. Yet, I still didn't have the strength and courage to tell anyone. I lost a little of my identity each day that I stayed with him! My insecurities started to bury me. I didn't know my worth; I didn't even recognize myself. I felt broken and hurt, yet the gifts, money, and trips felt good to me. I used those things as an escape and to justify everything hurting me. The only thing that made me feel happy was the materialistic stuff. Soon, accepting gifts in exchange for my respect became a pattern.

I developed a heavy addiction to marijuana and alcohol. It was another escape for me to avoid the pain, getting drunk and high thinking it would all go away. I found myself in a dark place, and I allowed that spirit to take over me. I gave him the power to control my mind, something he never deserved.

My use of narcotics turned into me selling drugs. It was my attempt at trying to find ways to make things better, save my relationship, and gain more financial stability for myself so I could afford the finer things in life. I started focusing on getting my body together, hoping for a change and for him to notice me as someone he should treat with love and not hurt. Little did I know, I wasn't doing anything but creating more pain for me by wanting to see perfection in him.

As I stared at myself in the mirror, comparing myself to what he saw, more and more insecurities built up within me. I didn't like me; I didn't like the way I looked. I had boobs and no ass; no way I could compete with the video girls who were on the rise back them. I began getting frustrated with hustling because that wasn't me! Got myself into some dangerous situations, but God's covering me is what kept me here.

I kept wanting to see the good in him. Yet, the support, time, and attention he once gave to me in the beginning of our relationship had all but disappeared. Still, I ignored the red flags that were flying high. It seemed like his mistreatment of me was a joke to him, and sadly, it happened again...

"I CAN'T BREATHE! YOU'RE CHOKING ME!" I screamed as he forcefully pinned me against the wall and then pushed me to the floor.

This time, his abuse was done in front of my good neighborhood friend, who defended me. The fact that my neighbor witnessed it humiliated me.

I know you're probably wondering why didn't I leave, why wouldn't I tell someone, and why didn't I get help. Well, it's easier to ask these things and give advice when you're on the outside looking in. When you're actually in the situation, it's a different type of feeling!

I was more afraid for him than I was myself, though. You see, my family is crazy, and my father's friends are just as crazy. So, he wouldn't have stood a chance if they knew what he was putting me through. I didn't want that. I guess you can say I was a fool in love. I was embarrassed, humiliated, weak, and didn't have the strength, courage, or confidence. I just couldn't do it. I couldn't find the strength to leave him.

Then one day, I reached my breaking point. I finally got tired of the physical and verbal abuse. Wanting my identity back, I decided to leave. I'd had enough and knew I deserved better, but I still made excuses for him while blaming myself.

As time passed, I have to admit that I started to miss our good days together. The shopping trips, dinner dates, and getaways. I missed all those things, but I was determined not to go back to the disrespect and abuse. I didn't necessarily miss the person but rather the benefits I received from the person.

The bible says you are fearfully and wonderfully made
But I'm questioning God like why am I feeling betrayed
But really, am I the only one to blame?
I'm in church every Sunday
And back to reality the same come Monday
I'm wrestling my insecurities
Not knowing my own abilities
Is this really the life that was meant for me?
Keeping everything bottled in
The fear that everyone would judge me
Would the critics critique me?
The church run and gossip about me
Would anyone understand?
Or would they say I'm a fool for staying?
Or would my story be the story that everyone is saying
Not to heal or help another nor me
But to destroy and cause more clutter, you see
Just continue to hinder me
Something the church would use as tea
I'm not even going to take the chance
I'm now looking at my life at a glance
There's purpose in your pain
I'll forever celebrate that saying
Don't let the spirit of fear mute you
You're worth more than this
Use it; that's a great gift
Take a stand; someone needs to hear from you

You never know who you might inspire through this
There's purpose in your pain
You'll never understand
Sometimes it's not just for you but also the next man!

VI

The phone rang, but I contemplated answering it. Sure, I missed him; however, I didn't deserve him. I deserved better. Some time had passed, though. *Maybe he got his act together. Maybe he's changed,* I thought. After two missed calls, the phone began to ring again.

"Hello."

"Hey, Stink. Wassup?"

I agreed to meet with him so we could talk. His attitude was different, and it seemed he had finally gotten himself together. He apologized for what he had put me through, and we both professed our remaining love for each other. *Maybe we just needed that time apart. Maybe this can work,* I considered.

As time passed by, he began staying with me many days throughout a week, and months later, the dynamics started to change. In the beginning, everything felt great like it did back when we first met, but as soon as I got comfortable and believed things were different, he started exhibiting his old behavior. He would come over but then leave back out and stay gone until one or two o'clock in the morning, and sometimes even later than that. For a while, I didn't say anything out of fear, remembering what happened the last time I questioned him about something. I was also aware that he was involved in hustling, so I didn't put much thought into it. I found myself sweeping everything under the rug again and becoming accustomed to the finer things of the world once more. One night, I got up the courage to question him about his late-night outings, which were increasing in consistency. Before I knew anything, I had a gun pointed in my face.

My heart stopped, and I blacked out. I just knew I was about to die. I could handle him choking me to the point where I was barely able to breathe, but if he pulled the trigger…

Scared, I trembled inside while silently crying and praying for God to spare my life. On the outside, I portrayed an image of not being afraid, refusing to show any signs of weakness. I'm stronger than that. Even when I've been weak, I've always remained in my strength.

Once he felt he had gotten his message across, he placed the gun under his pillow, rolled over, and went to sleep. Terrified, I couldn't go to sleep, not that I wanted to. How could I feel comfortable enough to close my eyes after he had just pulled a gun out on me? I was shocked, spooked, and didn't know how to respond to this.

I'd had enough. I couldn't take any more of his abuse. Him pulling a gun on me was enough to make me leave. Sure, he didn't pull the trigger that time, but what if I had stayed? Would there had been a next time? If so, would I have been able to walk away alive? As I worked toward building myself back up, I ignored all calls and texts from him because I was too nervous to have any contact with him.

Since I was afraid of what people would think of me, I kept much of what I was going through bottled up inside me. I didn't want to subject myself to being judged for my imperfections and getting unsolicited advice that wouldn't help me with my situation. I felt no one would understand. I can recall overhearing the conversations of women as they talked about domestic violence and being in those types of relationships. *That could never be me. If it was me, I would leave,* they would say. Then there were the ones who would say, *Oh, hell no! I would fight back.* As I sat back listening to them, I wouldn't say anything because I remembered I once had that same type of attitude. I never thought it could be me until it actually became me! I was only nineteen years of age at the time and didn't know how to handle this. A person doesn't know what they will do until they are actually in the situation. And for that reason, I decided to keep what I had been through to myself.

October 2010, my mother started commenting about my boobs getting bigger. Having been top heavy most of my life, I jokingly brushed her off.

"What, Ma? No, they aren't. They're the same size."

Then it was like something dawned on her. "Kiawana, you are pregnant!" she blurted out.

Those were the worst three words I could have heard at that point in my life!

"YOU ARE PREGNANT!"

"What!?! No, I'm not, Ma! Why would you say that?"

"We're going to get a pregnancy test," I remember her saying instantly.

Keep in mind, my mother didn't know anything about what had happened between me and my ex-boyfriend. Only nineteen, I was scared. What was I going to do with a baby? Then I thought about having to tell my ex that I was pregnant, and I started to panic. *He's going to kill me! He doesn't want to be with me, and a baby is only going to make things worse for me, not improve things. God, how could this happen?* The fact that I was getting Depo shots made me question how I even got pregnant. Thousands of thoughts ran through my head as I tried to make sense of it all.

My mother and I went to CVS, and after returning home, she watched me as I took the test.
Then we both patiently waited for the results. A horizontal line appeared in the small window of the test stick followed by a vertical line going down the middle, forming a plus sign.

Tears streamed down my face. What may have been perceived as happy tears were actually hurtful, broken, scared tears. *How can I be pregnant? No, there's got to be a mistake!*

But, there was no mistake. After countless urine pregnancy tests, some bloodwork, and an ultrasound, it was confirmed.

"OH MY GOD, I'M PREGNANT!"

VII

"We need to talk. I'm pregnant," I announced to him after dialing his number.

We were expecting our first child, but it definitely wasn't what I had planned for my life...not yet. Without a stable relationship or having a chance to establish a career, I didn't see myself fit to be a mother. Besides, becoming a single parent wasn't the most desirable situation for a nineteen-year-old girl to imagine. Yet, abortion wasn't an option for either of us. So, it looked like we were going to have a baby.

As if I wasn't already dealing with enough, I learned that my child's father had been sleeping with my neighbor for about three months prior to me finding out I was pregnant. The first trimester of my pregnancy I struggled with carrying immense emotional pain. Despite the front I put up, I was deeply broken on the inside. I could barely sustain, but I knew I had to stand strong and maintain for the sake of my child.

I'm pregnant. Gosh, I'm pregnant! I had to constantly remind myself of this because it was so hard for me to believe.

Finally, I got to the point where I accepted my situation. I wanted to be able to love with no regrets. There's nothing like a mother's love, and I wanted the best for my child. I thought maybe I would be able to heal, that my baby would help strengthen me so I could be a better version of me. I vowed to myself to be the best mother I could be to my child.

The day finally came when I would learn the gender of my baby. My mother, who never judged me, turned her back on me, or left my side after finding out I was pregnant, accompanied me to my doctor's appointment. We waited patiently for my doctor to come in. The whole time, I was fidgety and anxious, ready to know the sex of my child.

Finally, the doctor came into the room and began performing the ultrasound. He stopped midsentence while chitchatting with my mother and said, "Guess what, Ms. Leaf. IT'S A GIRL."

Instead of celebrating the fact that I was having a girl, I instantly silently prayed to God and asked Him not to allow my daughter to endure the pain that I had experienced thus far in my life and to keep her from falling for any toxic relationships. I prayed she wouldn't ignore any red flags that would possibly be shown to her in the beginning as I had done with her father. I prayed for God to give me the strength and wisdom to teach her what to never ever accept as a woman and to never settle for nothing than what she deserved. I prayed that He would help me to be the example of a phenomenal woman and that my daughter would grow up to be better and wiser than me. Lastly, I prayed for a change. In spite of all the pain I had endured from her father,

I asked that God would allow my daughter the privilege of being a daddy's girl!

I finally graduated cosmetology school and was in the homestretch of my pregnancy. However, with only two months left until the birth of my daughter, I started having complications and found myself in and out of the hospital. I wondered what was going on with me and worried if my daughter was okay.

The pain became intense, unbearable. At this point, I became concerned mentally, physically, and emotionally. The damage had been done in regards to my relationship with my child's father. Yes, my heart was still broken, but it was no longer about me. My main focus was our daughter. Still, it was a hard pill for me to swallow. The emotional pain of having to learn to forgive someone who isn't even sorry is hard, and it's even more difficult when you have a child with them.

My doctor placed me on bedrest for the remainder of my pregnancy. At the time, my doctor didn't know what was going on with me, but he informed me that if I continued to have complications, I would have to have a caesarean. My due date was originally July 29th, but with plans of a cesarean, they moved up the date to July 15th. If she were born on that day, our birthdays would be exactly one month apart. My little Key!

After many visits to the hospital because of constant pain and having numerous MRIs and ultrasounds performed, they finally discovered what was wrong.

"Ms. Leaf, theres a cyst on your ovary that your baby is kicking, which is why you're in constant pain. Also, we found a cyst on your baby's brain. With a cyst being on your ovary, there's a possibility we may have to remove your ovary, which may make it difficult for you to get pregnant again in the future."

CYST?!? BRAIN?!? OVARY?!?

God, what are you doing to me? How much more can I take, and what else are You going to take me through? I don't think I can stand anymore through this! Haven't I been through enough already?

I silently fired off question after question at God, hoping he could hear me. I didn't know how much fight I had left in me. I was tired, hurt, broken, stressed, depressed, and disappointed. Even worse, I was starting to question my faith.

VIII

It's time! It's time! I was thrilled, nervous, and afraid at the fact that I was about to give birth and would officially be a mother!

During my entire pregnancy, I put on a front while enduring the pain of my relationship. I was getting ready to have a baby by the man who had pointed a gun at my face. Never once did he apologize for any of the hurtful things he had done to me. But, I couldn't concern myself with that. I had to build myself up; I needed my strength to raise our child. Each day, I prayed that God would give me strength and rebuke the spirit of resentment that resided within me. I didn't want to create a strained relationship between my daughter and her father.

"Ms. Leaf, only one person can come back with you. Are you ready?"

Lord knows I only wanted my mother in the delivery room with me!

"Do you want your boyfriend to come back?" the nurse asked, waiting for me to respond.

"I'm sorry, that's my daughter's dad," I quickly replied with a hint of attitude.

Knowing it would be the right thing to do, I agreed for him to be there with me during the birth of our child.

After I kissed and hugged my family that was there at the hospital, they wheeled me to the delivery room. Princess Azariah was on her way!

After giving me an epidural, the doctor performed the incision that would welcome my baby girl into the world! Once my doctor cut Azariah's umbilical cord, he searched for the cyst that had been causing me pain. They couldn't believe it! They could no longer see the cyst that had shown up on the ultrasounds.

"Ms. Leaf, no additional surgery will be necessary. We can't find the cyst anywhere. It is completely gone. This is weird to me."

The doctor was in a state of disbelief, but not me. My Father up in heaven hadn't forgotten about me here on Earth! It isn't weird; it was a miracle. That's the healing power of God!

In the midst of one of the worst times of my life, I gave birth to a beautiful baby girl. I felt blessed with the gift of life that I had been given, but still confused, curious, and broken, I knew I was in for a fight.

God, what are you taking me through, and why are you taking me through all of this? Father God, why me?

IX

Not only did the love of my life turn on me, but I now had to raise our newborn daughter who looked just like him. The constant flashbacks of the arguments and fights, images in his phone of different women, having a gun pointed in my face, crying spells, feeling insecure and alone—all these things and more made me feel unattractive and uncomfortable in my own skin! Did my emotional state and feelings of unworthiness have to do with postpartum depression or was I experiencing PTSD?

This wasn't my plan. This wasn't the way I wanted things to be. *God, if this is your plan, I really don't understand, but take full control. It's all in your hands,* I would pray. Knowing that my battle was bigger than me, I tried to rebuild my faith and trust in God, fully relying on Him.

One morning, I woke up and proceeded with my normal routine of washing my face, brushing my teeth, and flossing before getting in the shower. But, as I looked in the mirror, I noticed a change in my appearance. The left side of my face seemed different and felt numb. I was unable to blink my eye, smile, move my mouth, or do anything on the left side of my face.

Already battling insecurities and being self-consciousness, I refused to leave the house until I was able to see my doctor. Sunglasses became part of my daily accessories, and I tried not to talk to anyone, afraid they would notice something was wrong. I constantly checked my reflection in the mirror, wondering if things would magically return to normal with my face just as it had abruptly happened to me. But, when nothing changed, I began to cry uncontrollably and question God, *Why me? Are you watching over me? Why am I going through so much? Are you even listening to me?*

My appointment day with my doctor finally came, and what I was told rocked my world.

"Ms. Leaf, you have Bell's palsy."

"BELL'S PALSY!" I yelled, never having heard of such.

"It's a sudden weakness in the muscles on one half of the face, facial paralysis," my doctor explained.

"PARALYSIS!" I yelled and began crying.

Everything else he said after that went in one ear and straight out the other. *How can I be paralyzed on one side of my face? This can't be real! How long will this last? Will my face go back to normal? God, why me?* I felt as though I was being punished but couldn't figure out. *Are you there, God? DO YOU HEAR ME?*

Last thing I recall my doctor saying to me is, "Whatever you are stressing about, let it go. Stress can trigger this. Everything is perfectly fine with your health, and your lab results came back normal. It's not worth it. Let it go. Stop worrying and stressing!"

LET IT GO, I wanted to scream. *Doctor, you have no idea all that I'm battling, and you're telling me to let it go! Let it go! Let it go! Yeah, okay, easier said than done!*

Suicidal thoughts, what is life to me! Having an abusive mate who cheated on me with my neighbor, a bad breakup, becoming a single parent, not feeling pretty enough, bouts of depression, and now facial paralysis. This is not at all how I imagined my life would be, and I seriously considered ending it all. Suicidal thoughts started to plague me as I searched for even a glimmer of happiness.

I was angry and upset with God, who I felt knew my heart better than anyone else. No one knew my entire story, all my insecurities, and now He gave me one more thing to deal with. *God, how could you!* I started to feel like God had abandoned me; He couldn't hear my cries! The only thing…or should I say the only one…who kept me here was my daughter, Azariah.

Many wondered why I would never put my daughter down, why she was always on my chest. Because having her close to me like that was the only way for me to rest. Azariah barely slept in her crib and seldom did I put her down for tummy time. She was breast fed almost until the age of two. My daughter and I have a different type of connection. She's the best part of me, and without her, I don't think there would still be a Key! She's the only one who makes me feel whole; she's all that makes sense to me in this crazy world.

Six weeks later, my daughter and I went to the doctor for a checkup, and everything went very well. I had regained the full function of my face. That Sunday, I decided to go to church, and everyone was excited to see me. Well, they were more excited to see Azariah! All the attention was on her, but I didn't mind one bit!

After church service, I saw my co-pastor lingering at the front of the church. I wanted her to see my daughter, but I also needed to speak with her and ask for her to pray with and for me. I was dealing with so much and didn't know how much more I would be able to take. I just wanted to be reassured that God hadn't forgotten me! As I tried to get her attention, she literally walked right past me as if I were a ghost!

I stood there in shock. To be totally honest, I was hurt. Wasn't she supposed to be a leader, my co-pastor, my inspiration, and my guidance to Christ. So, as I left church that day, I was still asking myself the question, "Why me, God?"

X

It's my 21st birthday! After attending a pole dancing class with my girls and going to a pink and white affair that had just let out at the Gaylord, where my godsister had gotten us a room for the weekend, my girls and I were hanging out in the lobby .

A group of three guys walking by caught our eyes. They stopped, and we began talking to one another. I blamed the alcohol for making me a social butterfly that night. Because I had been pregnant and was breastfeeding, I hadn't indulged in any alcoholic beverages in about three and a half years. Also, I was still dealing with the trauma of my daughter's father putting a gun to my face, so I didn't trust anyone. I'd been single ever since we split up and had no romantic interest! Yet, I found myself instantly drawn to one of the guys. I was captured by his brown skin, long locs, and nice lips that he constantly kept licking. We exchanged numbers, and the rest was history.

As time went on, we started spending a lot of time together, and as a result, I started catching feelings for him. It was 2012, and it had been almost two years since I left my daughter's father. I believed I was ready to date again.

It feels amazing to be able to talk with and vent to your significant other like they are your best friend. I opened up to him about a lot but didn't share EVERYTHING with him about me. We developed a dope bond that I just knew couldn't be destroyed. I truly believed he was meant for me and that we were meant to be. Or was it me trying to trick myself into thinking that this thing between us HAD to work, especially after everything I had gone through in my previous relationships. Since I hadn't totally healed from the past, I started to question whether pursuing something more serious with him was really a good idea.

I wasn't sure, but what I did know is what I felt with him was refreshing and rejuvenating. I wanted to be with him; I wanted a relationship. Sure, I was hesitant about committing myself to another man. The thought of being touched, not having trust, and possibly having a repeat of my past situations in my new relationship created an unspoken fear within me. But, something about him made me willing to take that chance. Or could it be I was so broken that I was looking for anything to fill the void? Following my heart and not my mind, I let the worry fade away and allowed myself to get so wrapped up into him that I eventually began falling in love with him.

Everything was great for the first two years that we dated, but after that point, those feelings of being refreshed and rejuvenated began to diminish. I wanted more, but he seemed to be afraid of commitment. Him being a firefighter didn't help. You know how some women can be when it comes to a man in uniform. With so many women giving the chase, I guess it was hard for him to resist the temptation, which left me feeling like it was a competition to win his heart. I slowly saw myself regressing back to the dark mental state I was in before I met him.

Then, I missed my cycle. At first, I shrugged it off as me just being stressed and it affecting my cycle, but after another eight weeks had passed by with still no cycle, I figured it was time for me to take a pregnancy test. I prayed for the results to be negative. No way did I want to be pregnant and possibly end up being a single parent twice over.

I finally placed the call to him. "We need to talk."

After we met up, I broke the news to him that I was pregnant.

Immediately, he responded, "Key, I'm not ready for a baby. I'm not ready to be a father."

His response didn't come as a surprise to me, but it still left me wondering what I had done so wrong in my life to deserve so much pain at such a young age!

While looking out the window, I quickly tried to wipe away the tears that were streaming down my face so he wouldn't see me actually crying. At that point, all I could do was pray to God and ask Him to forgive me for what I was about to do.

The decision had been made for me, and we were at the clinic. As I waited for my name to be called, he tried to lighten the situation by attempting to make me smile, but I couldn't find anything funny at that moment. When they announced they were ready for me, I was taken to the back, but this journey I would have to face alone since he couldn't come with me. I began crying uncontrollably and couldn't seem to stop. I felt even worse about what I was getting ready to do. I already believed God was punishing me, and after this, no way would He still love me.

The nurse spoke, interrupting my thoughts. "Ma'am, if this isn't what you want to do, don't do it. No one can force you to terminate your pregnancy."

Yes, you're right, I thought to myself, *but who's going to be there with me at three or four o'clock in the morning to help with a hollering baby and a two-year-old who won't go to sleep? No one will be there to help me financially, and it's already a struggle for me!* So, with no answers to the plenty of questions regarding my future with two children, I did what I felt I needed to do.

During the ride back to his house, I couldn't stop crying. I stared out the window while trying to portray an image of strength, but in all reality, I felt enervated with life. I didn't think God understood me. Now, after a few years of not dating, I thought I was ready only to end up right back here.

Dear God,
Can you hear me? I feel you left me. I have endured
so much pain and don't feel you understand. I know
you were with me when a bullet could've taken me
out, but I feel you left me shortly after that. It seems
you've gotten tired of giving me chance after chance
after chance, and I still haven't gotten it together.
You may not be pleased with my life, but neither am
I. God, I just wonder do you still love a sinner like
me?

After this, I didn't date or get too close to another man.
I didn't take anyone seriously. Instead, I just played the game.

XI

It was the year 2015, around Valentine's Day. During this time, my best friends and I had become big fans of a local band and were literally at all their shows, which took place Thursday-Sunday. Eventually, they decided to add another band to join them in performing at their shows.

I immediately took an interest in the new band's guitar player. I'm not a musician; however, I'm in tune to music, and something about that instrument just does something to me! The guitar! Its sound is amazing and soothing; it's everything to me!

He was shorter and different than my normal type. A Chinese and Jamaican mixed, he was a red-bone, had a curly bush haircut, and a gorgeous beard. I was feeling his vibe the whole night. By the end of their set, I was giving one of my best friends the eye. I would never approach a male who I was interested in; it just wasn't my thing to be the pursuer. But, with him, it was different. It had been a year since my last situation, so I only wanted to have some fun. However, I wasn't quite sure I was ready yet.

Still, the two of us exchanged numbers that night and kept in contact. I continued to go to just about every show. It didn't take much time for us to start going out, spending time together, and learning each other.

The things he would share with me made me want more for him. I always pushed him to step outside his comfort zone, and truthfully, I think I wanted it a little more than he wanted it for himself. Over time, he asked for me to be with him as a couple, and pushing my fears aside, I agreed. He was living with his cousin at the time, sleeping on their couch. So, after making it official, we decided to move in together. Because of his bad credit, we agreed I would put everything in my name, and he would take care of the rent. I would be responsible for utilities and groceries.

Everything was going beautifully. He had talked about plans of marrying, and before I knew it we were going ring shopping. Time progressed, and he asked for my hand in marriage. Of course, I said yes. After all, isn't it every girl's dream to be someone's wife.

Finally! I was finally experiencing overall joy in my relationship! Soon, I found myself busy with wedding dress shopping, meetings with my wedding planner, and my bridesmaids in order. I was excited, but I did find myself wondering if I had only said yes because I wanted to be his wife or if I was only caught up in the idea of being married and having a beautiful wedding. However, just as quickly as I questioned myself about the reasons why I had accepted his proposal, I convinced myself that I was more than deserving. I considered everything I had been through and believed that this was who God had for me. I could see us together for eternity. I only hoped he felt the same.

Moving ahead, our relationship became shaky. He lost his job, but his story as to the reason why seemed fictional to me. Then, his daughter's mother started calling me wanting to talk. Once we got engaged, it seemed all types of attacks began to hit us. I asked myself, *Is this a sign? God, is this not who You have planned for me? Is this my confirmation that I said yes for all the wrong reasons?*

His daughter's mother came to our house and informed me of many things about my fiancé that I had NO idea about. Some stories he had shared with me, but she explained them with a different twist than what he had told. As I listened to everything she told me, things began to make sense. Not because of what she was saying, but because I had heard the same from others, as well. *My God, what have I gotten myself into?*

Enraged, I called him, wanting him to come home that very second. I'd had enough of being embarrassed. I also called my best friends and told them to meet me at my house. After all, I didn't know what was about to happen.

Having a big heart and trying to be there for others can sometimes be to your own detriment, seeming to torment you more than anything. It was then that I realized I was starting to become what and who hurt me; I was becoming that toxic person. I never properly healed from my previous damaging relationships nor had I forgive myself. Living with regret, I used this relationship as a crutch to get over what had hurt me, thinking it could work. Now, all that was bottled up inside me would be released towards him.

As I waited for my best friends to arrive, I blew his

phone up, constantly calling, screaming, cursing, and threatening him. He claimed he was out applying for jobs and take his resume to different employees, but honestly, I didn't know what he was actually doing while driving around in my Lexus. The mother of his child had informed me that he never had a license. So many petty lies had been told to me, and I felt like I didn't know my fiancé at all! The last call I placed to him, I threatened to call the police and report my car stolen if he didn't come home within five minutes.

My best friends made it to my house before him. By this point, with so much built-up anger, hurt, and frustration, I was annoyed.

When I heard his key in the lock, I charged toward the door, and with every bit of strength in me, I swung at him with both fists, catching him off guard. He stood bleeding and confused with a dumb look on his face, probably wondering why his daughter's mother and my best friends were there. I wasn't certain of where he had been, but it seemed as if he had already gotten into a fight prior to me putting my hands on him. But, I couldn't concern myself with that; I had my own pain to deal with.

I'm not sure exactly why I was standing there crying; I assume they were more so angry tears than anything from the feeling of having my heart being used and abused. I felt humiliated, embarrassed, and disrespected. I'd wasted my time and money being with him and was beyond enraged. A few days before meeting with our wedding planner, I called off the wedding. My fiancé who I thought I knew I really didn't know at all. I found this out when I asked him questions based on what his child's mother had told me, and he confirmed much of it was the truth.

I received another shock when I started getting eviction notices on my door and learned my fiancé never paid our rent. Seemed the notices had been coming for a while, but he threw them out before I could see them. That's how far behind we were on the rent. Praying my daughter and I would still have a place to stay, I went back and forth to court to plead my case and ask for mercy along with some time to get the money for the past-due rent. I learned that the lame had been stealing money that I had hidden around the house and taking money from my daughter's piggy bank. He had also been lying to me about where he had been so that he could spend time with his daughter's mom. On top of that, he was stealing equipment from the church where he worked, which resulted in him losing his job. The most shocking and hurtful of all the things I learned and heard about him were the rumors of him participating in sexual activity with men. How much more could I take?

In order to deal with all that I was feeling, I went back to using marijuana and drinking heavily. I literally would smoke six to eight joints a day, if not more, to aid with my pain.

You may be asking yourself, why am I so open? Why am I so willing to share so much of the darkness of my life? It's because I want you to see where God has brought me. There is so much more could share, but I don't want to get too intense nor do I want you to feel sorry for me. What I want is for you to try to understand and see what God has done for me! How His miraculous hand was always covering me even when I felt He forgot all about Key.

XII

I managed for five years taking care of my daughter with the help of my supportive village — my mother and stepfather — as much as they could. But, I'd had enough of struggling. I wasn't the only person who created my child, so why should I have to foot all of the responsibility? It was time that I file for child support since her father refused to willingly provide financial support, and that's exactly what I did. After going back and forth with him, and his broken promises to help, I felt I had no other option.

"Based on the statement of your earnings that you've provided to the court, sir, you are hereby ordered to pay one thousand dollars a month in child support. Another court date will be set. At that time, both parents will need to bring copies of their two most-recent paystubs," the judge said.

I never imagined my life would be like this, and it was beyond frustrating. Why couldn't he just take care of his child instead of being forced by the courts to do so?

He worked for his friend's tow-truck company, and of course, that friend looked out for him by fixing his paystubs to reflect less than what he was actually making on the job. So, when we returned to court, instead of having to pay me $1,000/month for child support, his payments were reduced to less than $450/month. And he couldn't even be a man a pay that regularly. He would pay between one to twenty dollars here and there, and once in a blue moon, he would surprise me by sending a hundred dollars.

I wanted to throw in the towel and give up. It was not fair that he was able to come in and out of her life as he pleased, while inconsistent parenting wasn't an option for me. No matter what he did, I had no choice but to make ends meet!

Despite what I was dealing with, I refused to be one of those parents who took their frustration out on their child. Sure, I felt a little resentment at the fact that I was left to raise the child of someone who wasn't even sorry for what they had put me through. And yes, my anger and frustration left me feeling like I wasn't the best mother I could possibly be to my daughter. But, I would not project the way I felt about the father of my daughter onto my child.

Although I barely grossed $25,000 annually, the government said I made too much and therefore could not receive government assistance. How could they say I made too much when for me, it was nowhere near enough? I wanted to give my daughter a good life like I had while growing up. I wanted her to experience the privilege of a private school education, while receiving love, respect, and support from home.

With the weight of so much on my shoulders, I had trouble sleeping and experienced bouts of depression. My doctor prescribed me Zolpidem to help me through this test.

Father, I'm crying to you. Heal me, free me, strengthen me, and break this chain off of me. Give me the strength to be able to forgive. Help me to forgive someone who's not even sorry. Help me to forgive them with not just my mouth but with my heart, as well. Father, I need you. Rescue me. Set me free.

That became my daily prayer. I wanted to be released from the bondage and pain I'd been holding on to. I felt so broken that I kept myself captive in that spirit and couldn't see a way out.

My daughter's kindergarten year at school wasn't the best; my baby struggled a bit. I wondered if the cyst on her brain that the doctors found during the sonogram had returned, or was I the one to blame because of all the pain and emotional abuse I endured during my pregnancy? I even started blaming her teacher, saying she didn't know how to teach my daughter and wasn't showing patience. I wonder why the Board of Education hadn't fired her after receiving so many complaints about her teaching or lack thereof. I don't know why, but there was an underlining animosity between that teacher and I throughout the school year. The crazy thing is my daughter's teacher had known me since I was my daughter's age, if not younger, and is someone who I considered like family since she was the mother to the nieces of my mother's best friend. This only left me more baffled as to why she would treat my daughter in such an uncaring manner.

On my daughter's graduation day from kindergarten to the first grade, her teacher crossed the line when she grabbed my daughter a little too rough by her arm. Seeing this, my mother asked to speak to her in private and addressed the situation. I thought it was resolved, until the teacher started causing a scene once back in the public eye. Her demeanor suggested it was NOT resolved and that she wanted to settle it as if we were out in the streets handling a beef. She used a lot of hand motions, sarcasm, and disrespectful body language while speaking in an elevated tone. The teacher criticized and spoke of my daughter's weaknesses in front of my family, friends, and complete strangers, which wasn't any of their business. Enraged, I charged towards the teacher, ready to beat her ass, but my family and friends pulled me back before I could get my hands on her.

During a meeting with the school directors and my co-pastor, they put the blame on me. My co-pastor even went as far as to label me an animal because of the way I reacted. They found no fault on the teacher's part; all fingers were pointed at Kiawana. No one wanted to address what had provoked me. When it comes to my child, though, there is no limit on what I'll do to protect her. Children are strictly off limits, but most importantly, mine is not to be played with! No longer would I respect the person who showed my child no respect. That was enough for me.

A few weeks after my daughter's graduation ceremony, the police showed up at my door.

"Is Kiawana Leaf home?" they asked my stepfather.

My mother called to ask me where was I since I wasn't at home. Not wanting to wait around for me to return, the officers left with the promise to came back another day. When they did, I stalled coming to the front door. I couldn't figure out why they were there, and the last thing I wanted was to have a run-in with the law again.

When I finally came to the door, I saw one of Kennedy's finest standing there. Officer J is what I called him. I felt a little more at ease but was still puzzled as to what he wanted with me?. He asked me to step outside, and when I did, that's when he proceeded to ask me if my daughter's teacher's name sounded familiar. I laughed while informing him that of course I had since she was my daughter's school teacher. My curiosity piqued even more at the mention of her name.

"Wow! Interesting. I don't know what you did to that woman for her to fear you," he stated sarcastically while chuckling, then handed me a manila envelope.

I opened it to see a temporary restraining order inside.

I burst into laughter. "Are you serious? I really have to go to court for defending my daughter? Is this some kind of joke?"

Someone who was like family to me and who would see me at family gatherings actually filed a restraining order against me! I guess the joke was on me for thinking that she wouldn't.

The day we appeared in court, there were so many familiar faces from the church which we both belonged to that I felt like they automatically sided with her instead of caring to hear my side. Funny thing is, I had made numerous calls to the church, school director, and the co-pastor to explain what had happened, but I couldn't get a return call from any of them.

Even though the judge dismissed the temporary restraining order, my daughter's teacher requested for us to return to court for a permanent order to be put into place. Can you believe this?!
So, guess what? Yep, you guessed it. We were back in court again!

This time, she was alone with the exception of her husband, who was a police officer. She showed up with a crutch and a limp. I'm assuming she was trying to play on the judge's sympathy. Although I'm sure he knew–just like I did– that it was all an act.

Despite her theatrics, the judge saw no reason for a permanent restraining order and ended up dismissing both orders. It is then that I began to resent church. In my time of need, no one from the church showed me any support or acted like they even cared, and that hurt me the most. So much finger pointing from the pulpit, but what if it had been their child? Would they not have protected their child...or acted as an "animal" as they said about me.

Till this day, I have never received an apology from my church, not a phone call nor a home visit from any of the members. *Judge not lest ye be judged,* they say. Yet, they seemed so quick to judge me without knowing the true story.

After this, I didn't want to go to church even though it was LITEARLLY all that I knew and where I had been brought up. What once felt like home to me now felt like a foreign place. The pastor was supposed to be my leader, but what example were they really displaying? Instead of feeling uplifted after church service, I left there still feeling the heaviness of hurt and bitterness of betrayal. Soon, going to church just became a routine to me. I was only there because that's what my mother instilled in me.

XIII

My life battles were intense and seemed to be never-ending. I still carried hurt from my abusive relationship and tried to stomach the pain from my broken engagement. Then there were the rumors that I had to face of my ex sleeping with another man, along with the stares and whispers from those who knew. All the while, I struggled to try to forgive myself from my previous poor decisions when it came to relationships. I fought for my daughter; I fought to give her a normal life, while barely making ends meet and trying to keep a roof over our heads. For the most part, my life consisted of going back and forth to court for child support, holding grudges, resenting the church, carrying toxic feelings, and asking God why my life had to be filled with so much chaos and pain.

Still, I tried to live my life being strong and smiling while carrying the world on my shoulders, never displaying all of the pain that I was really in. People thought they knew me, but they really didn't know me in the place that I was in.

Mentally, I wanted to break down and throw in the towel. I still struggled with depression and thoughts of suicide, and medicated myself with alcohol and marijuana. Despite wanting to talk to someone, I didn't think I could stand getting rejected by those who wouldn't understand what I was going through . So, I chose to keep it all bottled up inside, hindering myself from healing and remaining toxic.

Just about every party that I attended with my friends, I found myself running into my ex fiancé. Of course, all my suppressed resentment towards him would resurface. If I couldn't get my money, I wanted blood. I had invested too much in him and lost too much while we were together. I was still trying to recover from him damaging my credit, so no way could I just let it go.

I soon became the abuser instead of being the victim. I found myself once again becoming like those who had hurt me. It became a pattern for me. Every time I saw him, I would sweet talk him as if I wanted him back just so I could get him alone with me. I would text a few of my friends to make sure they were watching from a distance and would have my back if things got out of hand. That's when I would unleash my anger on him, striking him and daring him to hit me back. I would take the little cash he had on him, but that still wasn't enough for me. My friends would be my eyes, letting me know his whereabouts whenever they ran across him. As soon as I caught up with him, I would repeat my act of luring him in and then taking what I felt was rightfully mine.

This same scenario played out for at least six more months until I eventually grew tired and took it for what it was…a loss.

XIV

On top of everything else, I was still going through a hectic battle with my daughter's father. He'd randomly call, expecting to get her even though I already had plans for me and my daughter. When he couldn't get her, he would let some time go by, about two or three months, and then pop back into her life but doing the same thing as far as not giving me advance notice when he wanted to see her. He showed no consistency when it came to our daughter, whether it was regarding financial help or spending time with her.

Soon, I started receiving threatening text messages from him, such as "I bet I'll get her from school, and you'll never see her again."

Because of how he acted during our relationship, I never took his threats lightly. In fact, I never underestimated *anything* he said. When the messages became more frequent, I decided to file for full custody. That way, the court could set a visitation schedule, and that would hopefully cut down on any future issues.

"Ms. Leaf, your daughter is almost six years old. What took you so long to file?" the mediator asked me. "Is everything okay? Are you or your daughter in any danger? What's happened that has you fearing this man?"

I'm hesitant to reply. *Do I lie? Do I tell the truth? Do I really want them in my business? Will they judge me? Will they call the police and make me relive my situation? Will it only make things worse? Am I even ready to face my truth?* Many thoughts clouded my head.

"No, ma'am," I finally responded. "I just constantly get text messages from my daughter's father threatening to kidnap her when things do not go his way. I get no financial support from him, and he doesn't even spend any time with her."

After all the paperwork had been filed, I was informed I would receive a letter in the mail once a court date had been scheduled.

With a credit score that hit rock bottom, a savings account with no savings, barely able to afford the basic necessities, and carrying toxic hurt from numerous failed relationships, my world was gray. My life was in shambles, and it seemed like everything that could possibly go wrong did.

Shackles shambles
Something more like a gamble
Scramble?
That's what life seems like
You knew my name but never my story

It's daily life, but no one ever talks about the fight
We bottle it in, like to front, fake, and pretend
A change has to start within
I wish this existed back then
A voice that needs to be heard
I'll start it off about mine

Part II
"Beginning of Healing"
XV

2017

Once my childhood best friend passed away, I felt an urge to get closer to God. One promise I vowed to her at her gravesite is that I would walk in my purpose so we would be able to see each other again in heaven. Church was one of the main things missing from my life. Wanting to fill that void, I visited my male best friend's church in Virginia. It was a Hispanic church, so their way of worshipping was something completely different for me. But, the atmosphere, people, worship, and presence of God was so authentic. I liked not knowing anyone or having to worry about judgement, side-eyed looks, and whispered conversations about me behind my back.

During church service, I found myself laid at the altar

with tears streaming down my face. I cried out to God, asking Him to remove the toxic thoughts and lessen the weight of my burdens. I begged for His forgiveness and for Him to strengthen me, help me, and guide me. With my eyes still closed, I saw a bright whiteness then experienced a cool sensation followed by a hot feeling. It was almost as if the toxicity was being burned out of me; it also felt like someone was standing over me during all of that. I didn't know what was going on or the exact meaning behind what I experienced, but it moved me to start weeping hysterically.

After I stood to my feet, the ministers embraced me while praying over me. They repeatedly told me that I was healed and free. Having never personally experienced God or the feeling of the Holy Ghost before, I wasn't sure exactly what they meant and wondered how they could be so certain about what God had done for me if they didn't know what I was going through. I know what I wanted, but I still didn't feel as though I was healed and free. However, the feeling that I felt was surreal. I felt the extra weight lifted off; it was unusual, but I knew it was nobody but God.

After service, we met my best friend's friend, who's a faithful member of the church, and she told me, "It's not time for you to have a boyfriend. God says you're healed and free, but He wants you to do what you are supposed to do."

What am I supposed to do? Do what exactly? Yes, I knew I wasn't living completely right, but I didn't put too much thought into what she told me. Instead, I chose to ignore the fact that God was actually speaking to me through her, possibly wanting me to fully trust and rely on Him,

Whenever I was in church, I felt incredible and free. However, once I walked out those doors, I returned to my reality and was back doing everything as once before, staying in a toxic place and keeping myself in bondage! In spite of her telling me it wasn't time for me to have a boyfriend, I still ended up in unhealthy situations and left trying to heal myself afterwards.

One morning after dropping my daughter off at cheerleading practice, I decided just to drive around to kill some time. While cruising around town, I blasted the song "Crazy" by Micki Miller. It was as if she was singing the lyrics for me.

When I was broken, you came and saved the day
Changed all my forecast, you made my heart behave
When I was hopeless, you took my stress away

As I sang passionately along with Micki, tears began to fall down my cheeks. I'm not sure who her lyrics were meant for, but for me, I was speaking to God when I sang the words. I began praying and being completely vulnerable, transparent, and honest with God. I asked Him why was so much happening to me and failing me. It's the first time ever I heard God directly speak to me.

YOU HAVE TO HEAL BEFORE I CAN BLESS YOU.

Thinking I was hallucinating, I turned down my music and wiped the tears from my face. Again, I heard the exact same words.

YOU HAVE TO HEAL BEFORE I CAN BLESS YOU.

I sat in both awe and confusion. When I thought of hearing from God, I imagined hearing a deep baritone voice. But, the voice actually sounded like my own.

Each time I thought I was making progress–growing and removing toxic things and people from my life, I would backslide and find myself right back in my mess. It was like the devil had a strong hold on me. I would go right back to using marijuana, drinking alcohol, and associating with people who were not good for me.

The following day, I went to brunch with a longtime friend. I was having a hard time accepting that Kay was gone, and the grieving process was not easy for me. In fact, it has been the hardest process ever in my life, and I'm still trying to find ways to cope with the pain. Well, by the time we left from having brunch, I was drunk. Once in my car, I smoked a jay. I was completely gone; I wasn't even aware of myself. Having never experienced a high like that, I started to wonder if something had been slipped in my drink while at brunch, or had the marijuana that I smoked been laced? Normally, I have a high tolerance whenever I'm drinking or getting high, but this time was nothing normal for me. Something just didn't feel right.

I followed my friend to a secluded residential area, and I got into his truck after we parked. Some things about that day are a little blurry for me, but what I do remember is him taking my pants off and fingering me roughly. It was the most uncomfortable feeling I'd ever encountered. It felt as though I was losing my virginity all over again. I was so intoxicated that I didn't put up a fight, though. It was like I was under the influence of a date-rape drug.

To my relief, his phone rang, and after answering the call, he told me that he had to go. Was that God saving me? Were His angels protecting me from being taken advantage of by him? Who knows what the outcome would have been had he not received that call.

As I stumbled from his truck, I blurted out in my slurred voice, "I'm unable to drive," but he seemed not to be concerned about my safety at all as he pulled off. Once I made it back to my car, I got inside, locked the doors, and passed out.

Next thing I knew, I was parked in front of my house. But, like most people who drink too much and then drive, I had no idea how I made it there in one piece and without any damage to my vehicle. I still felt terrible. This certainly wasn't an ordinary hangover. I started vomiting and had diarrhea, feeling as though I had some type of food poisoning.

When my best friend came over my house later that day, he was talking on the phone to the same woman from his church who had prayed over me. In complete amazement, I realized that everything she had said was true, but how did she know so much? Once again, she told me, "God said you are healed and free," but this time, she added, "You have to believe it for yourself, though." Question is, was she referring to my life as a whole — mentally, emotionally, and spiritually?

Momentarily, the vomiting and bowel movements ceased, and I felt physically better. But, before long, I was back at it. I couldn't eat nor drink anything. By six o'clock that evening, I decided to go to the emergency room. Along with the same symptoms I had been experiencing, I was dehydrated and lightheaded. While awaiting the results of the bloodwork and tests, I was given medication to stop the vomiting and diarrhea. Finally, the doctor came in.

"Ms. Leaf, you have gastritis. Gastritis is inflammation of your stomach lining. In order to reduce flare-ups, you'll have to change your diet and lifestyle."

My Lord! What could possibly happen next?

XVI

2018

Before the New Year, I vowed to start going back to church and grow closer to God. First, I had to find a church home that would help with my spiritual growth, challenge me, and provide the support I needed. I still struggle to understand why God would take Kayla away. Yes, we got the opportunity to repair our friendship but not rebuild it, and that really bothered me. Fighting a battle to stay clean of drugs and alcohol while trying to cope with the loss of my friend among other things, I finally turned everything over to Christ, hoping to gain a clearer understanding. Before 2018, I began visiting House of Healing and Zion Landover. I felt the intense presence of God during each and every visit, especially at House of Healing.

I reached out to Pastor Battle via Instagram, and the fact that he responded meant a lot to me. However, because of my unpleasant past experiences with church leaders, I was hesitant to get close to any pastors. So, when he did reach back out to me, instead of running towards him for guidance, I shied away.

House of Healing declared that 2018 would be the year of manifested dreams. As a little girl, I dreamed of owning a hair salon. However, over time, I lost my passion for cosmetology. I completed cosmetology school during the worst stage of my life but wasn't motivated or interested in it any longer. Instead, I became more focused on becoming the voice for others who have experienced the same things I have, but I wondered if I would be able to do so successfully.

Some told me, "Kiawana, you have a story to tell. You never know who your story might inspire and help heal." Although I battled with insecurity, fear, doubt, and not wanting to be judged by others, I thought maybe I could host different empowering events not just for others but for myself, as well. I felt it would help me to fully accept my past, be able to talk about it, and help heal, inspire and empower women to embrace our vulnerability instead of being ashamed of it. So, I stepped out on faith, and in October of 2017, I became the business owner of InspiHer, LLC.

On November 11, 2017, I held my first seminar focusing on domestic violence. While attempting to share my story, I found myself too startled to speak in regards to being a victim. However, as I listened to the testimonies from other women, I know I was not alone. Still, I started to question whether being a speaker was what God called me to do. In other words, was this my purpose?

One Sunday at House of Healing, the co-pastor laid hands on me and told me the same thing I'd heard before! *You are healed and free, but you have to believe it and have faith in God to receive it.* This made the third time I'd heard the exact same thing. Such a coincidence! Or was it?

I believed the message was indeed coming from God. Maybe if I worked towards accepting and believing what had been spoken over my life—not once but three times— things would change and I would finally understand. So, I began changing my walk in life and the way I thought. I stopped smoking, accepted myself for who I was, embraced my humility in order to build my confidence, and forgave myself for the errors of my ways. I spoke forgiveness not just with my mouth but also from my heart. Releasing grudges I was holding regarding myself, I started letting go of toxic pain and broke the chain of bondage off of me. It was a step towards being completely healed and free.

Through my spiritual growth, I wanted to get more connected with the Word. I began reading daily devotionals from the You Version bible app, plans I felt concentrated on areas that were a struggle for me. One scripture stuck out to me.

Galatians 1:10 – *Am I now trying to win the approval of human beings, or of God? Or am I trying to please people? If I were still trying to please people, I would not be a servant of Christ.*

Repeatedly reading this passage, I asked myself, *Am I trying to get approval of humans or God? Am I keeping myself in bondage by seeking acceptance from people, or do I firmly believe that God has forgiven me to be accepted by Him? Do I fear judgement from people or God?* From there, I embraced the reason of forming the organization – to help heal, inspire, and empower women who experienced the same situations that I did of battling burdens, pain, fear, and toxicity while having no outlet or inspiration. Why keep all of that bottled up inside when I could use my trials to help inspire someone?

I wanted to be an example to others that you don't have to have a certain image in order to be connected to Christ. No matter what our flaws are, God still feels we are worth saving. God will still use us, and He loves us all the same. I wanted to help other women develop self-love, remove toxic things or people from their lives, inspire them to know there's purpose in their pain, and to realize the things that keep us in bondage, not allowing ourselves to heal and progress forward. My story isn't the only one that can help, inspire, heal, and free another. Yours can, too. This just doesn't apply to women but men, as well. My desire was for us as a people to come together to encourage and support one another. However, I wasn't certain if I was able to handle this responsibility while still trying to cope with my story.

It seems everyone would rather glorify the negative ways of this world. Instead of running towards Christ, they are more concerned with worldly things. When you're toxic, people celebrate you, but when you grow and heal, they would rather not be connected with you. Grow and heal anyway. It was hard for me to accept that some people would rather see me down bad than thriving, but I still chose to grow and heal.

January 8, 2018, I attended House of Healing, and Pastor J prophesied that God called me to be an entrepreneur. I had so many excuses as to why I wasn't ready. How could God call someone who didn't think they were qualified for a calling? I didn't think of myself as being healed, so how could I minister to someone else about getting healed? I was still flawed and not financially ready. Sure, I launched InspiHer, but could I handle the responsibility of what I was called to do?

XVII

While people go through life trying to grow, forgive, and let go of hurt, the devil is always busy killing, stealing, destroying, and wreaking havoc in the world. My havoc came in the form of my daughter's father, who filed to have his child support payments modified. As we stood in the courtroom, he downed my name, blaming me for the loss of his job, and gave a sob story as to why he was unable to pay the amount of his court-ordered child support payment. The judge ended up honoring his request to have the payments lowered, ordering him to pay seventy-five dollars a month.

How is one expected to take care of a child while only receiving seventy-five dollars a month?

I didn't know why I entertained circumstances that I had no control over. Why continue to shed tears of frustration over things I could not change, only hurting myself more? Why let things that I should be accustomed to affect me? Why entertain evildoers when God has never failed me? Has my daughter ever gone without? No. Is my daughter hurting for anything? No. Yes, I sacrificed a lot, but God always made a way out of no way for me and my daughter! Why continue to give him power that he didn't deserve?

During this same time, I was blessed with an opportunity to be on TV One's "For My Man". I auditioned to be an extra on the show but was declined for every role. Then, almost two months later, they reached out to offer me the lead role. The role was about a young woman who fell deeply in love with a man who was in and out of prison, had multiple children with him, developed a cocaine addiction, and assisted him in doing home robberies. Although not my exact story, it reminded me a lot of my life story. When I compared my life to the story of the lead role, it made me realize what God had done in my life and how far I had come. But, He wasn't done with me yet.

XVIII

The atmosphere in Zion was relaxing. It's where I could be myself. I didn't have to feel like anyone was watching me or worry about being judged because I didn't wear floor-length skirts or church suits. It was a relief not to have to fear being criticized if I didn't lift my hands in worship. Nor did anyone show any judgement at the sight of my tattoos or comment about why I was crying when the spirit moved me. This is something I loved about Zion and House of Healing. I didn't fear judgement. Both churches were inviting, and if I needed anything, I knew I could reach out to the pastors without fear of being rejected or denied.

Because Pastor J could just pick up the phone and call me, I stopped attending House of Healing. It got too intense for me; I didn't think I was ready. Whenever he would text to check on me, I'd give him some excuse for why I wasn't in church. Truth is, I was afraid of moving forward in my spiritual growth. Pastor J held me accountable, and I just didn't feel capable of handling that type of responsibility!

Sunday after Sunday, the sermons began to speak directly to me. Although I had asked God for clarity of my calling, I don't think I was ready for what He began to reveal to me through His Word. I wasn't in denial but rather disbelief. The sermons challenged me. For every excuse that I came up with to run from my calling, God would use the pastor's sermons to speak directly to me and try to get me to understand.

One Sunday, Pastor Battle's topic came from Matthew 13:31 and was titled "What God Can Do with A Mustard Seed." **The Plan** was his first point. He described "The Plan" as being the seed – your dream, your vision.

Okay, I'm with you, I thought to myself. My seed is the idea, the concept, my platform, my testimony. InspiHer is my dream. It's my vision.

"You must plant the plan," Pastor Battle preached. "Sow into your own dream!"

Okay, God, you lost me a little with this one. Plant the plan; sow into your own dream. Yes, I stepped out and started my LLC, but I am still uncertain if this is what I am supposed to do. What qualifies me for this calling, especially when my life isn't right?

"**The Process** is the time during which God grows you in the dark. He will give you your vision in the dark. That's growth. Don't abandon the process!"

I'm in awe. Everything Pastor Battle is saying is perplexing to me. I feel like my life is still in the dark, and I'm still in a hurtful place. I haven't completely healed or freed myself from my past hurts. I am still in the process of growing closer to God. Is "The Process" the stage in which I grow and heal?

"**The Purpose** is NEVER about you. It's about the people that you're going to help! Surrender to the process that will help bless others!"

MINDBLOWING! I'm going back and forth with God, but He's coming right back at me. Okay, Kiawana, this isn't about you. Yes, your life is in the dark but that's a part of your process. You will grow from this place where you are. God has called you for a reason at this exact time and place where you are in your life. This isn't about you!

As much as I tried to convince myself of that, the truth is I didn't want to be called. I wanted to live my life on my terms. It was like playing a game of tug of war, a battle between good (spiritual growth) and evil (worldly ways).

I didn't feel like I was ready for this journey to begin. So, I stopped going to church. I decided I would rather go to brunch or just spend the Sunday at home.

Why? Why can't I just be me, Lord? I prayed. But, the thought and visions would never just let me be. It was as if my dreams were tormenting me.

XIX

One Tuesday, my best friend asked me if I wanted to go with him to bible study at House of Healing. I gave him every excuse I could think of to try to get out of going, but he wouldn't take no for an answer.

During bible study, Pastor J went into depth about defining dreams.

"**Timing Defined** is a point when something particular happens. **Dreams** are given by the Holy Spirit and used to burn your spirit to push you to move out of your comfort zone."

Even though I had stopped going to church, dreams still appeared to me. The dreams showed me ways to deliver my story and how to use my business. Since I choked up whenever I attempted to talk over a mic, my dreams told me to release a book in order to share my story.

As I continued listening to Pastor J, he preached, "Something is getting ready to roll into your life that's going to feed your dream! Desperation can provoke a movement from God. This is the season to make impactful moves! God's assignment will never be for your arrogance."

I heard everything he said but lacked understanding. Anxious, I wondered what would happen to feed my dream. Every time I went to church, the messages delivered always seemed to focus on dreams and purpose, which started making me depressed since I couldn't figure out either. *And impactful moves? What moves could little ole me make that would be impactful?* I found myself struggling with this assignment and started to believe the message wasn't for me, as anything that forced me to face my fears would also require me to get out of my comfort zone. I wasn't quite sure I was ready for that.

Then, I remembered...*2018–the year of manifested dreams!* How could I make this possible for me? Remember, I had no new aspirations since losing my passion for cosmetology, and after my childhood best friend passed away back in July of 2017, I became desperate to find my purpose before my time was up on this earth. While reflecting on my life, two words I'd heard Pastor J mention several times while preaching kept reverberating in my head.

Manifest: to make clear or evident to the eye or the understanding; show plainly; to prove; put beyond doubt or question.

Dream: a succession of images, thoughts, or emotions passing through the mind during sleep; an involuntary vision occurring to a person when awake; a vision voluntarily indulged in while awake; daydream; reverie, an aspiration; goal; aim. *(According to Webster's Dictionary)*

Once I considered what these two words meant to me in regards to my life, I instantly began to have chills!

In the midst of my mess
I thought God only qualified the best
He put me through a test
To help heal the next
When I say heal, I don't mean just physical sickness
But toxic drugs, addictions
Insecurities, lust, broken pieces
Hatred, burden, generational curses, more so the bitterness
Denying my faith, I began to go astray
Too far gone, quickly trying to find a way
That's normally how it's made
You're introduced because that's what mommy teaches you
Maybe even a grandmother, too
But, turn away due to how the world consumes you
Battling real-life crisis
Different outlets or medias would suffice
Influenced by the world
Where all that's promoted is sex, money, and drugs
Hurt by the church, I rather not turn to that
Who can I trust? Who would lead me towards my best?
To forget for the moment
Sex, drugs, and money will be my aid
In the midst of my mess
God qualified me for the next
But, I don't think I'm ready for this test
How can I change for the best?
He qualifies the call

He doesn't call the qualified
In the midst of a mess!
You know how the saying goes
Only God can turn a mess into a message
A test into a testimony
A trial into a triumph
A victim into a victory
All in the midst of a mess!

XX

I'm in my process! Yes, there are still periods of tug of war with me, and I'm still not completely clear of my mess. However, I'm not as deep in my mess as I once was before.

One Sunday at Zion, Pastor Paige gave a sermon (from Genesis 30:25-32) on the topic "Spot Cleaning." He shared with the congregation how he didn't want to respond to his calling, how he would rather go out drinking and partying than host bible study night. He'd rather fit in with the crowd than stand out and answer God's calling. Listening to his story gave me a glance at my own life. *Perfectly imperfect with blemishes and spots!* But, how does God call one to be used in spite of their flaws?

"You want dark spots to change, and at the same time, you need dark spots in order *to* change," Pastor Paige preached. "You can't handle getting clean without having the blemishes to begin with. You can't change without God. Change is not easy!"

Pastor Paige was certainly preaching to the choir with that message.

Pondering this, it began to get personal to me. *God, you still love me that much to even be used by you? You have a purpose, promise, and plan for me! You see so much more in me than I can see in myself!*

I began wanting to desperately work through the troubled areas of my life. By remaining stuck in my past, how much pain was I actually causing myself? Reliving being broken, vulnerable, resentful, bitter, and my experiences of chaos, betrayal, drug addiction, and toxic relationships with men only kept me in that place of hurt. While I was drowning in the darkness of my pain, those who hurt me in my past were probably sleeping peacefully like they didn't have a care in the world or concern for what they had done to me. Continuing to carry dead weight resulted in no one hurting besides me. I knew releasing my pain wasn't going to be easy, but it was necessary if I wanted to free myself. Why keep myself captive and remain toxic? God is a merciful, graceful Father. He had already forgiven me. So, why couldn't I forgive myself?

In the meantime, I'm cleaning my spot through my process, spiritually developing a stronger relationship with God like never before. I took the step to become a member of House of Healing, and I'm praying more. Not only do I pray for myself but also for anyone who has hurt me. More than anything, I ask that God bless my daughter's father and free him of whatever may be hindering him. After all, we have to co-parent, and it wouldn't be healthy for me to carry resentment towards him for an eternity. My daughter is what's more important to me. During my spot cleaning, I fast, eliminate social media, and disconnect myself from toxic people. Things I've never imagined myself doing intensely! I've accepted that I can't change on my own; I can't do it alone. So, I desperately seek God's help. Now, I'm feeling happier, glowing, evolving, and growing by getting closer to Him.

It's hard to connect with what once excited me and the people who excited me! From experience, I've noticed that people only celebrate you, love you, and want to be around you when you're toxic, weak minded, vulnerable, and have no self-identity. They feel you're easier to abuse and control when like that. From the depths of my heart, I prayed for God to remove the toxic people and things from my life that are not of Him. Quickly, they were revealed and removed from me. Relationships became disconnected, friendships grew distant, and casual conversations were non-existent. Those who I thought were for me are no longer near me. Those that were around during this toxic stage of my life are no longer interested in me. No one wants to celebrate this healing process with me, and I'm okay with that. It seems it's harder for people to accept this new and improved Key. It's a battle, but I know it's what's best for me. People are quick to talk about what's happening in the world, nightlife, and gossip, but if I broach the subject about religion and church, there's crickets. Reflecting back on Galatians 1:10, I had to ask myself, *Am I trying to win the approval of humans or God?*

XXI

Another Sunday morning, I streamed Zion before going to House of Healing. Pastor Battle preached the topic of "The God Interview."

"Write down one question you are asking God right now," he said.

Wanting assurance that I was on the right path, I wrote, *When will I get clarity of my purpose?*

Through Pastor Battle's sermon, God spoke to me and said, *When you just do it!*

Easier said than done, I thought to myself.

Pastor Battle went on to say, "You think you went through what you went through for you, don't you? Do you think you conquered test, trials, and tribulations for nothing? Nooooo! God did that to use you. Whatever it may be, He took you through it for a reason. You are to share your testimony with someone else so that you can inspire them. God will get the glory for what he brought you through! Your purpose is never for you nor about you. So, get out of thinking everything is about you, you, you! It's not about you!"

After hearing this, I started gaining confidence, strength, and a better understanding. Facing my fears, I became desperately hungry to manifest this God-given assignment (dream) to reach my destiny. I didn't know what God had planned, but I knew it was bigger than my wildest dreams. My vision and dreams were much clearer to me, and it was no random coincidence!

My bible app verse of the day was Hebrews 10:35. "So do not throw away your confidence; it will be richly rewarded." I couldn't let social media or those of the world control nor influence me any longer. It doesn't bring awareness to what is real. People are in pain and suffering all over. Most people are living their life for LIKES, living a façade, and hiding behind false images instead of accepting their need for healing, whether it be physically, mentally, or spiritually. Social media will tear your confidence down and tempt you to be disobedient to God as you seek approval from man. Your purpose isn't going to be accepted and understood by everyone, but if you've build your confidence to accept that, it won't matter to you! Build your faith and put your trust in Him. If your purpose doesn't intimidate you, that's not your God-given assignment. I'm getting there.

Blessed with another acting opportunity to be in the documentary *No More Chains 2*, my faith started to pay off. Breaking chains of bondage and breaking generational curses, I began seeing my purpose clearer. Every door that opened and opportunity that God blessed me with, all came back to His calling and the plan He had for me. As I looked back on my life and how far God had brought me, I remembered Pastor J saying, "Something is getting ready to roll into your life that's going to feed your dream. Desperation can provoke a movement from God. This is the season to make impactful moves." I wondered if my new acting opportunity was that something. I became desperate; God significantly moved in my life; and I began to make impactful moves in the season I was in.

Things never happen when you want them to or when you expect it. God moves on His time, but always remember He has a plan and promise for you! One of my downfalls is rushing God's plan and wanting to do things on my time because I'm anxious to get it done. One thing I can definitely say with confidence is, faith without works is dead.

You can't live the same way and expect something different. God will not bless you with His purpose and plan for you if He sees no change in you. You can't experience real happiness without experiencing Him. You have to change your life, but you can't do it alone! A new lifestyle is a process, not an outcome. You must focus your energy on building better and not becoming better just to see a result. Strive for permanent change instead of just changing for the meantime. I was determined to take my relations with Christ to another level in 2018. I couldn't expect a change in my life while still living the same routine way.

XXII

Are you going to walk in purpose or fear? It's a question I asked myself constantly. So, I'm asking you the same... *Are you going to walk in purpose or fear?*

Back in 2017, my hasty response would've been, "I'm walking in fear, but want to find and walk in my purpose!" Through my spiritual growth of trusting God and applying His word to my life, I began taking steps towards developing a different level of courage and confidence. Nothing great would come from living in my comfort zone. Therefore, I had to walk in faith while facing my fears and insecurities, and firmly believe I am an overcomer just as God sees me. However, it's not as easy it sounds!

We've all faced a difficult situation at some point in our lives, whether it occurred when you were a child or is something you are facing right now. In the midst of your storm, you must trust, obey, and believe in God. Your ability to overcome will not come from your strength alone. Don't treat this temporary time as if it's a permanent defeat. Be the victor and not the victim! God doesn't make you go through anything that is not in His plan and that He knows you will not overcome.

A lot of times we hinder ourselves from growing and healing by living in our past. "LET IT GO!" We cannot change what has happened. We cannot go back and fix what has happened. We cannot undo anything from our past. What we can do with our past is evolve, grow, learn, and heal from it. Embrace and accept your past! Living in the past does nothing but keep you from living in the present and planning for the future. "LET IT GO!" I know you're probably thinking, "Yeah, Key, that's easier said than done." Well, I had the exact same attitude, and nothing happened for me but a repetitive cycle by holding on to the past. It always played in the back of my mind and held me captive. Trust me, it will be the best decision for you. I promise!

Don't live with regret and always find it in your heart to forgive. Even if someone who wronged you never apologized to you, forgive them. Forgive them with your heart just as God has forgiven you. I'm sure you've heard it before that forgiveness isn't for the other person but for you. Forgive them in order to release the toxic animosity that has a hold on you. To heal, grow, be free, and happy, you need to forgive!

And let me say this…happiness isn't found in things, people, or money. Happiness is found within you. Money can't buy you happiness. Yes, with the right amount of money, you'll be able to purchase things that will provide temporary happiness, but it won't remove the toxic things in our life that already reside there. I became addicted to retail therapy, but it only took my mind off of everything for the moment. Trying to fill the void in your life with materialistic items will not make you complete. Once the adrenaline I experienced while shopping disappeared, the reality of my life was right there staring me in the face. The type of therapy that is good for you is heart therapy, healing therapy, and therapy sessions with God where you sit down and pour your heart out to Him. No matter what you face, always keep yourself first, and make sure you are healed and happy within before attempting to find it in someone else.

XXIII

My pain was God's way of punishing me. I truly believed that. When we experience pain internally, we know it's a sign that there is a problem. When I experienced vomiting, drooping facial features, and pain during my pregnancy, I knew there was sickness in my body. When something is physically ailing us, we go to the doctor to figure out what is going on and to hopefully be healed. Those who battle with depression and anxiety turn to doctors for pills to ease their symptoms and help them cope. When I was going through my personal battle with depression that prevented me from sleeping because of my racing thoughts, my doctor prescribed sleeping pills for me. What if we turn to God for a cure? What if God allows us to experience pain in order for us to turn to Him for healing? But, that's actually what He does. He has us go through certain trials and tribulations so that once we overcome the situation, we share our testimony of what He has done so that we can help heal others.

A lot of times, we think the term "healed" correlates with sickness, i.e., something is physically wrong with your body and needs to be "healed". However, that is not always true! This was why I struggled with understanding when told I was healed and free or that I had to heal before God could bless me. I knew what I wanted (to be healed), but didn't feel it. I still felt the pain (sickness) inside of me. I didn't understand what I needed to do exactly to get to the point of feeling healed and free! God knew what was going to happen; He was just waiting for me to desperately seek Him and not anything else. He had already done His part before I actually felt it for myself. He had already forgiven me and wiped away my sins!

2 Corinthians 1: 3-7 (New Living Translation) "All praise to God, the Father of our Lord Jesus Christ. God is our merciful Father and the source of all comfort. He comforts us in all our troubles so that we can comfort others. When they are troubled, we will be able to give them the same comfort God has given us. For the more we suffer for Christ, the more God will shower us with his comfort through Christ. Even when we are weighed down with troubles, it is for your comfort and salvation! For when we ourselves are comforted, we will certainly comfort you. Then you can patiently endure the same things we suffer. We are confident that as you share in our sufferings, you will also share the comfort God gives us."

There is purpose in your pain, and there is a reason why I keep saying it. It is written there is pain in your life for you to be used by God. God wants us to desperately chase after Him for healing rather than seeking comfort from money, drugs, and engaging in fornication. Thinking the pain will go away if we ignore it won't work. Thinking we can handle it on our own won't work. Whatever you use to numb the pain inside of you won't work! It just gives the situation more power and control over you.

God uses our problems to achieve His intended purpose. THERE IS PURPOSE IN YOUR PAIN!

God doesn't intentionally cause pain or suffering in our lives. Never look at what you are going through as a form of punishment, even those things that may have happened to you as a child. Instead of asking God why you, have you ever thought *why not you*? Jesus Christ died on the cross for our sins so we could be right with God.

2 Corinthians 5:21 "For God made Christ, who never sinned, to be the offering for our sin, so that we could be made right with God through Christ."

However, our suffering is actually discipline. This is the testing of our faith that produces endurance. James 1:3 says, "For you know that when your faith is tested, your endurance has a chance to grow." Therefore, I encourage you to be joyous through your trials.

Through everything, He will always be there, and at the right time, you will understand His plan. Always remember that God has a bigger plan for you than you have for yourself.

(Here are a few scriptures that inspired me through my trial of healing and gave me assurance, desperation, hope, and closure. I hope they will inspire you, as well.)

Psalm 147:3 *"He heals the brokenhearted and binds up their wounds."*

Psalm 34:18 *"The Lord is close to the brokenhearted and saves those who are crushed in spirit."*

Ephesians 1:10 *"And this is the plan: At the right time, he will bring everything together under the authority of Christ — everything in heaven and on earth."*

XXIV

When I look back on my life, I firmly believe this is the right time to share everything that He planned for me. I will use my tests as my testimony to share with and help inspire others. I will turn my trials into triumphs and my mess into a message. Instead of being a victim, I will celebrate my victory. I have no one but God to thank for everything. I now have a better understanding, even for those days when I felt He was punishing me. Everything is coming together for me; my heart is pure. I can finally say I am healed and free. I have my own identity; I don't need validation or approval from anyone. Doors are opening for me, and opportunities are presenting themselves. My co-parenting relationship is getting a little better. But, most importantly, my relationship with Christ is much stronger!

2 Corinthians 12:5-10 became my favorite scripture, directly relating to my life. *"I will boast about a man like that, but I will not boast about myself, except about my weaknesses. Even if I should choose to boast, I would not be a fool, because I would be*

speaking the truth. But I refrain, so no one will think more of me than is warranted by what I do or say, or because of these surpassingly great revelations. Therefore, in order to keep me from becoming conceited, I was given a thorn in my flesh, a messenger of Satan, to torment me. Three times I pleaded with the Lord to take it away from me. But he said to me, "My grace is sufficient for you, for my power is made perfect in weakness." Therefore, I will boast all the more gladly about my weaknesses, so that Christ's power may rest on me. That is why, for Christ's sake, I delight in weaknesses, in insults, in hardships, in persecutions, in difficulties. For when I am weak, then I am strong."

All of the physical abuse done to me and that which I had done to myself was the thorn in my flesh, messenger of Satan, tormenting me. Three times I pleaded to God to take it all away from me, asking Him to heal me from the toxicity in my life and free me from my own captivity. This scripture made me understand the purpose of my pain *and* my life. How could I talk about God's power if I hadn't experienced Him for myself through my weaknesses? How could I inspire, encourage, empower, and help heal others without having first experienced God's power for myself? How could God heal me and call me into destiny without understanding His power for myself?

Now I am transparent about my weaknesses and able to share my story without insecurities or fear. I don't boast about myself. I boast about God and everything He has done for me. Twenty-six began a new chapter for me to be completely healed, free, and allow my Confidence to Unlock!

Part III
"The PROCESS"

"I don't mean to say that I have already achieved these things or that I have already reached perfection. But I press on to possess that perfection for which Christ Jesus first possessed me. No, dear brothers and sisters, I have not achieved it, but I focus on this one thing: Forgetting the past and looking forward to what lies ahead, I press on to reach the end of the race and receive the heavenly prize for which God, through Christ Jesus, is calling us. Let all who are spiritually mature agree on these things. If you disagree on some point, I believe God will make it plain to you. But we must hold on to the progress we have already made." Philippians 3:12-16

Here I am now trying to live my life right for God, trying to fulfill my purpose. But, it seems every time I move forward I'm pushed further back. I get overwhelmed, frustrated, and start having doubts! The devil and his attacks are trying to control me and take me back to where I was but don't want to be again. It's easy to go back to what you're used to, but how would that help me get closer to being submissive to God? I'm not perfect, and I still make mistakes. But, I know what my goal is. How do I stand in front of others offering guidance while everything within myself isn't perfect?

"It is not that we think we are qualified to do anything on our own. Our qualification comes from God." 2 Corinthians 3:5

The point is God calls us to an assignment in the midst of our process of getting closer to Him. The hardest battle that I am fighting is to trust in God and not rush the process.

XXV

The main factor in any process is **TRUST**. Without trust, you're left with little to nothing. Trust can be delicate and challenging, which can create fear in a person. However, trust is one of the most important attributes of our walk with Christ. Trusting God and His process is the jewel to practice our faith. Many of us, including myself, fear trusting someone (or something) because of past experiences or we are unsure how to trust. The difference (and most amazing thing) is God is not man; He does not put us through a process that will kill, hurt, or destroy us.

"The thief's purpose is to steal and kill and destroy. My purpose is to give them a rich and satisfying life." John 10:10

Although you may know this, it can still be hard to trust that which we cannot see. This is where God actually tests our faith. He wants to see if our faith is strong enough to extend our trust to Him. When we fail to trust in Him, we only make life harder on ourselves. By not trusting in Him, we are taking the plan and purpose out of God's hand and placing it in our own.

At times when we have plans and expectations for ourselves, we become gullible and take the wrong path, leading ourselves on paths of destruction and becoming frustrated. This is exactly what the devil wants us to do. He'll make it where you lose focus or constantly hit roadblocks that make you want to give up on reaching your goal.

I learned this the hard way. I made the mistake of worrying about HOW things would happen instead of trusting that they would happen in the way God intended. By not trusting God, I was losing focus of God's calling over my life. This is why it is important to **TRUST** in Him.

"Trust in the Lord with all your heart; do not depend on your own understanding. Seek his will in all you do, and he will show you which path to take. Don't be impressed with your own wisdom. Instead, fear the Lord and turn away from evil. Then you will have healing for your body and strength for your bones. Honor the Lord with your wealth and with the best part of everything you produce. Then he will fill your barns with grain, and your vats will overflow with good wine." Proverbs 3:5-10

I'm curious, how will this all work out? It's just me! God, you called me to be an entrepreneur, but I have no resources or knowledge about entrepreneurship. Honestly, I am intimidated by the process of becoming an entrepreneur and all that it entails. But, after receiving this prophetic calling, why would I not trust His wisdom? I'm ready to go. It's time to hustle and get it done!

Why is trusting God important to Him? Why isn't the fact that we believe in Him not enough? Maybe it's because many put their trust in the world and what it has to offer, while very few put their trust in God.

Trust indicates our heart; it reflects who our loyalty and commitment lies with. During our trials, we are quick to rely on God. But why only in the midst of a trial or tribulation are we affirmed to trust in God? Just what if we are the cause of the difficulties in our lives instead of learning to put our trust in God? After all, it is clear to us: *"You must worship no other gods, for the Lord, whose very name is Jealous, is a God who is jealous about his relationship with you." Exodus 34:14*

XXVI

In addition to developing a stronger relationship with God, I also wanted to be in tune with Him. Knowing that I am unable to complete any assignment on my own, I had to grow and become mature with Christ. So, I decided to go on a spiritual fast for clarity, direction, and to be sensitive enough to hear God's voice. The fast consisted of prayer and devotional time and omitting television, social media, worldly music, fried foods, alcohol, and sweets for one month.

Early 2017, I had the desire to write a book about my testimony but would always start and stop, allowing fear to get in the way and not thinking I was capable of doing it. Still, in 2017 and early 2018, I continued to write not knowing how I would get it edited, published, marketed, or anything! With the many visions and ideas that I had for my story, I was instructed to create a vision board. I felt it was a quite a coincidence that every magazine I selected to use for my vision board seemed to include powerful quotes and images that related to my life story. Here are a few:

- *"Be Bold. Be Brave. Make Noise!"*
- *"What Are You Willing to Stand Up For?"*
- *"You cannot buy the Revolution. You cannot make the Revolution. You can only be the Revolution. It is in your spirit, or it is nowhere." (Ursula K. Le Guin)*
- *"I Love Letting People Know They Are Not Alone."*
- *"I Want Everyone to Feel That They're Worth Standing Up And That There Is Good in Our World!" (Oprah)*
- *"Knowing What Defines You Brings You Closer to Being Your Most Powerful!" (Oprah)*

Coming across an article in one of the magazines, it had several words written in bold letters. Two were relatable to my purpose and vision: CONFIDENCE and UNLOCKED. During my fast, I had dreams, visions, and signs of Inspire Too Empower. After repeatedly seeing this, during my prayer time, I consistently asked God for clarity. Should I change my business from InspiHer, LLC to Empower Too Inspire instead? I could envision the logo in my mind. The T would represent a cross and the word "Too" would be used as an adverb.

Where I was mentally with my plan and this fast, I was able to receive clarity on a lot that I battled with. During my prayer and devotional time, God gave me Jeremiah 29:11: *"For I know the plans I have for you," says the Lord. "They are plans for good and not for disaster, to give you a future and a hope."*

Being drawn to the words "Confidence" and "Unlocked" for a second time, I felt there must've been a plan for me to use those words as a title, but I just didn't feel it was the time for me to present my story to the world. So, with my brother's help, he connected me with a graphic designer, and I focused on getting the logo completed. I was sure God would let me know when to use it.

Once my fast ended, I continued writing even though I had to fight through the procrastination. Honestly, I didn't think I wouldn't actually release a book. Never saw myself as being an author, but I decided to keep writing and saved what I wrote just in case I ever took that step. Once I started to seriously consider putting my story out there, I DM'd a few colleagues on Instagram who I knew had released a book for assistance and guidance, but no one wanted to help. So, I decided to help myself and began searching the web for publishers and editors. Some raised a red flag for me. There were those who wanted you to invest money in order to have your book published and then there were the others who had bad reviews. Becoming discouraged, I prayed, "God, if this is Your plan, I trust You'll make a way." After saying that prayer, my focus turned to acting, but I never stopped writing, although I did procrastinate a lot during the process.

It was the second day of filming for Ari Squires' *No More Chains 2*. The documentary reflected on a lot of individuals that "empower too inspire". The successful men and women in the series faced many of the same traumatic life situations that I had faced: pain, fear, depression, addictions, and abusive relationships just to name a few. The characters displayed growth, showing it was time for a change and providing strength, courage, and inspiration through their stories to help others break free from their bondage. The whole time during filming, Jeremiah 29:11 constantly replayed in my mind.

God, I know that all of this is a part of Your plan, I prayed. *How blessed I am with the opportunity to be inspired by the purpose of Empower Too Inspire. I'm in awe that You dropped my name in Nicole Mason's ear for me to portray the younger version of her in this film. I fully trust You and know there are more great things to come as long as I trust in You!*

Little did I know how soon those great things would come into being. I connected with a member from my former home church who was also a part of the documentary. While speaking with her, she spoke highly of her publisher who was preparing to release her book. The publisher she spoke of was Ms. Charron Monyae, CEO of PenLegacy. I went from having doubts about releasing a book to God leading me to this phenomenal woman who could help me publish it.

Have you ever sat back and thought God has quite a sense of humor? You think of plans and then doubt yourself while He just sits back and laughs like, "Yeah, okay, I'll show you!" As God pushed me closer to my dreams and visions, I could no longer procrastinate about writing my story. I had to be sincere, focused, and get out of my comfort zone. I wanted my story to be an authentic, transparent, raw, inspiring, and encouraging account of my living testimony.

Now that You've aligned me with a publisher, God, it's time to move forward.

XXVII

Trust and faith play a big part when it comes to relations with Christ. The closer my relationship with God gets, the harder the devil attacks me. For example, I thought I had completed my book and texted my publisher with the exciting news.

After saving the file to my computer, I went go to use the lavatory. When I returned to my desk and tried to search for my manuscript to send to my publisher for editing, I got the following message: *Sorry, your file could not be found.*

Immediately, I started to panic. I attempted to retrieve my file several times, but the same error message continued to pop up. Angry and upset, tears flowed from my eyes and down my cheeks. Desperate, I reached out to a few computer pros that I knew to ask for their help, but the result was still the same.

Discouraged, perplexed, and still crying, I called my friend to vent. She was able to calm me down and offered encouragement, reminding me what God had called me to do. "Whatever you had was not all that God wanted you to say in the book," she had told me. "Stop, pray, calm down, and go back to it tomorrow."

When my publisher responded to my text, I informed her that I couldn't locate the file, and she offered me the same encouraging words as my friend. "Stop and pray," my publisher had said. "That draft wasn't going to be your best seller. Your next draft will be better than the first. Now, no more tears unless they're joyful tears thanking God for your best seller."

The following day was a Sunday; I streamed Zion Landover, and Pastor Jenkins was the guest preacher. His sermon topic was "I'm Not Going Down Without a Fight."

"The devil doesn't just attack any and everybody. He specifically goes after the ones he know are trying to do greatness for the Kingdom, the ones who understand the assignment that God has called over them, and the ones who give God the glory. That's who the devil attacks! He will do any and everything in an attempt to make you lose your trust and faith in God. The devil wants to block you from glorifying Him and making an impact in people's lives," Pastor Jenkins preached.

There will be moments of weakness that will test our faith and commitment to God, and boy did I have a few more moments. Chances are you will give in. After all, we are only human and not perfect. Flesh can consume you and guide you away from what God has called you to be or assigned you to do. However, do understand that you are held accountable! Will you continue to trust God and His plan even in the midst of a hardship?

"We can make our plans, but the Lord determines our steps."
Proverbs 16:9

The hardest part of my process and chasing my dream is trying to understand the signs that God sends. Is He giving me signs to stop, or is He testing my faith to see if I'll trust in Him and keep going? During this process, I'm hit with so many attacks that I strongly consider giving up, but my spirit won't allow me to do it because I know that's exactly what the devil wants.

I want to trust God's plan, but why am I struggling to believe God in the midst of what seems impossible? Could it be that I am actually making it harder for myself?

When I start to have feelings of doubt, I reminded myself of Pastor Jenkins' message about the devil not just attacking anyone. He attacks people who are destined to birth greatness for the Kingdom of God. So, I will keep going and fight. When I get tired, I'll step back, take a moment to rest, and trust in God to handle the rest! This process is definitely a fight, but I'm determined not to give up.

The anointing that's on your life attracts attacks! Don't look at it as trouble. Look at it as confirmation. KEEP GOING!

XXVIII

I have to be honest with you. As challenging as it seemed to embrace my vulnerability and live a life understanding my purpose, nothing topped everything I had faced during the process. Everything matters intensely to me now that I've found my true identity, my purpose. At the same time, it seems like I have the world on my shoulders, and no matter what happens the devil wants me to turn my back on my mission, my purpose. For instance, I received a phone call that my great grandmother was terminally ill and would pass away any day. With all intentions to see her, I wasn't able to make it. She passed away before I was able to tell her that I would see her later. I thought what else could possibly go wrong! With facing family sicknesses and conflicts with the startup of my business, I started to feel overwhelmed and like I wasn't meant for this.

Right when I thought about giving up, I spoke with a teenage girl who lacked self-confidence, feeling like she wasn't pretty enough, comparing herself to the other young ladies that she had seen on TV, and trying to live up to the standards of society. She reminded me so much of myself when I was her age. Little did she know, she gave me strength to keep moving forward.

A few days later, God used my best friend to speak to me to give me even more confirmation. She randomly texted me an encouraging message and sent me a few lines from Tweet's song, "Created for This".

> *"So many times, I tried to run away*
> *I couldn't find rest 'cause there was no hiding place*
> *And I heard a voice come up from deep within say*
> *This is who I am; I no longer can pretend*
> *And I was created for this!"*

I thought to myself, *Lord, there is no doubt in my mind that I'm chosen. You gave me a song to let me know it's okay to tell my story, and I owe you all the glory!*

I became very emotional. I needed this confirmation. Before then, I was feeling hopeless, discouraged, and like my back was against the wall. There will be times in your life when the devil will test you, but keep your faith and know that God will send you a gentle reminder that you have come too far to turn back now! I was created for this, and this is my Confidence Unlocked!

Empower Too Inspire

I pray through my story, *Confidence Unlocked*, that I was able to help and inspire someone. Understand that there is purpose in your pain. Be encouraged during your trial. Believe that you are more than enough, and don't settle for less. Love yourself. Grow, evolve, heal, be free, break free of your bondage, and forgive not only others but yourself, as well. Forgive yourself for falling into the all-too-comfortable behavior and patterns that contributed to the trials and tribulations you endured. Forgive yourself for being who you were in order to become who God wanted you to be. He has already forgiven you. God has a calling, plan, and purpose for your life. He is only waiting on you to realize it! What you go through is never just for you, but to use you to be a vessel unto the Kingdom — to help inspire, heal, and encourage another. We are the devil's biggest target! Can you imagine if we started a change within ourselves? To step out of our comfort zones and actually heal? We, both male and female, would be a force to be reckoned with together. I'm not trying to shove my religion or Christ on you. However, when you've experienced so many hardships and hurt, and have been healed of it all by Him, it's hard not to boast about it!

"Don't let anyone think less of you because you are young. Be an example to all believers in what you say, in the way you live, in your love, your faith, and your purity." 1 Timothy 4:12

129

Sister, you are not alone. I know the feeling of being afraid in a domestic violent relationship. But, PLEASE don't stay. Talk to someone. Don't brush your situation off as being something minor just because you only have a small bruise or maybe no physical scar at all. It's not something little. Abuse is abuse, whether physical, verbal, or mental. Don't let anyone tell you differently. Get help. What starts out as only a shove, slap, or name calling is oftentimes the beginning of things getting worse. And never stay because you don't feel anyone will help you. If no one else will help you, I will. I'm here for you! You are not alone!

Single mothers, I know it gets hard; it can get frustrating and overwhelming at times. It's a major sacrifice, but it's well worth it. No matter what, never allow anyone to take the credibility from you of being an impeccable mother! God wouldn't bless you with a blessing He didn't think you were strong enough to handle. There's no greater love than a mother's love!

As you embark on your journey to your "Confidence Unlocked" or work towards fulfilling your purpose, I encourage you to NEVER give up. Empower Too Inspire! Someone needs you.

With Love,
Kiawana "Key"

"I pray that God, the source of hope, will fill you completely with joy and peace because you trust in him. Then you will overflow with confident hope through the power of the Holy Spirit."

Romans 15:13(NLT)

About the Author

Life can be brutal, unforgiving, and beautiful all at the same time. For Kiawana "Key" Leaf, she's experienced this and a whole lot more. A self-made entrepreneur, author, actress, and inspirational speaker, Kiawana aspires to inspire and empower women who are survivors of domestic abuse through her first business venture, Empower Too Inspire LLC. The foundation of Empower Too Inspire is built on Women's Empowerment and Kingdom Advancement.

Kiawana is a rising star who was featured on TV One's *"For My Man"* and Ari Squires' soul stirring documentary *"No More Chains 2"*. While life has thrown many obstacles her way, Kiawana's faith in God has never wavered. She dedicated her life to Jesus Christ at the age of twelve. Kiawana's greatest inspiration comes from her greatest joy–

her daughter, Azariah. Kiawana looks forward to being an example to young women who are seeking spiritual growth.

CPSIA information can be obtained
at www.ICGtesting.com
Printed in the USA
JSHW011353151219
2922JS00004B/101